EXERCISES COMMEMORATING

THE

TWO-HUNDREDTH ANNIVERSARY

OF THE

BIRTH OF JONATHAN EDWARDS

HELD AT

ANDOVER THEOLOGICAL SEMINARY

OCTOBER 4 AND 5

1903

WIPF & STOCK · Eugene, Oregon

Wipf and Stock Publishers
199 W 8th Ave, Suite 3
Eugene, OR 97401

Exercises Commemorating the Two-Hundredth Anniversary of the Birth of Jonathan Edwards
By Richards, William Rogers, Platner, John Winthrop, Woodbridge, Frederick J. E., and
Smyth, Egbert Coffin
ISBN 13: 978-1-60608-037-5
Publication date 11/20/2008
Previously published by The Andover Press, 1904

JONATHAN EDWARDS

1703 - - 1903

THIS BOOK IS DEDICATED

TO THE MEMORY OF

EGBERT COFFIN SMYTH, D.D., LL.D.

CHRISTIAN SCHOLAR

THEOLOGIAN, HISTORIAN

PROFESSOR IN ANDOVER THEOLOGICAL SEMINARY

1863-1904

PREFACE

As the oldest Congregational school of theology in America, Andover Seminary esteemed it a duty, while she also counted it an honor, to celebrate the bicentenary of America's foremost theologian. Within her lecture-rooms the system of Jonathan Edwards has been diligently studied and sympathetically expounded. Her first professor of sacred theology, Dr. Leonard Woods, is commonly represented as a mediator between the two divisions of orthodox Congregationalism in his day, yet in substance he was a vigorous advocate of the Edwardean system, and his successor, Professor Park, was even more widely known as its interpreter. If Edwardeanism no longer controls the doctrinal instruction at Andover, the fact is due to no lack of reverence, on the part of her teachers, for the power of philosophical analysis and logical construction which has made Edwards famous for all time, or for the fundamental truths which he strove in thought to apprehend, but rather to causes whose operation no philosophical or theological system of the past is able permanently to withstand.

The aim of the bicentennial celebration was not merely to honor the memory of a great Christian leader, but also to attempt a discriminating estimate of the enduring value of his work,—an attempt which the lapse of time and the subsidence of dogmatic strife have at last brought within the range of possibility. Accordingly, in addition to representatives of her own faculty, the Seminary invited scholars of widely different antecedents, from outside of New England, to participate in the proceedings. The reader of the papers here published will observe differences in point of view which will at least relieve the record of monotony, and, it is hoped, will not detract from its value.

PREFACE

The celebration began on Sunday, October fourth, with public worship in the Chapel, where a large congregation gathered to listen to the commemorative sermon by the Reverend William R. Richards, D.D., an alumnus of the Seminary, now pastor of the Brick Presbyterian Church in New York. For the public exercises on Monday afternoon a distinguished audience was assembled, including a large number of alumni and other ministers from neighboring towns, together with professors from Harvard and from Boston University. The church had been handsomely decorated for the occasion, and portraits of President and Mrs. Edwards, loaned by Miss Park, stood on either side of the pulpit. Professor Day presided, and on behalf of the Seminary extended a welcome to the guests. By way of introduction to the more formal papers, Professor Platner sketched in outline the religious conditions of New England in the time of Edwards, after which Professor Woodbridge, of Columbia University, presented a critical analysis of Edwards's work as a philosopher. At the close of this session the invited guests adjourned to Bartlet Chapel, where a reception was held and supper was served. Many took advantage of this opportunity to examine the loan exhibition, consisting of the principal editions of Edwards's works, unpublished manuscripts and letters, and other objects of historical interest.[1]

Another large audience assembled for the evening exercises, at which Professor Hincks presided. The first address was a sympathetic presentation of the salient features of Edwards's theology by Professor Smyth, who was a life-long student of the subject. A poem, entitled "A Witness to the Truth," was read by its author, an Andover alumnus, the Reverend Samuel V. Cole, D.D.,

[1] A list of the most important objects exhibited will be found in Appendix II.

PREFACE

President of Wheaton Seminary. It elicited much favorable comment. An interesting feature of the program was the reading of a congratulatory message[1] from the Senate of the United Free Church College, Glasgow, which formed a suitable introduction to the closing address of the day, by Professor James Orr, D.D., of Glasgow, who spoke upon "The Influence of Edwards." The exercises concluded with a piece of ancient psalmody, sung by the congregation to the tune of St. Martins.

The memorial sermon, the poem, and the addresses of Professors Smyth and Woodbridge are here printed practically without change. Professor Orr's address is slightly enlarged. Professor Platner's address, which was not read from manuscript, will be found to vary somewhat from the form in which it was delivered. In Appendix I are printed extracts from hitherto unpublished notes by Edwards, collected by Professor Smyth in illustration of statements made in his address.

Thanks are due to Dr. Owen H. Gates for aid in correcting the proof sheets, and to Miss Mary W. Dwight for completing Professor Smyth's copy and for a careful revision of the proofs.

The sudden death of Professor Smyth lends a peculiar interest to the publication of this little book, for it contains the final labors of his pen. He had taken the deepest interest in the Edwards celebration from the beginning, and was earnestly desirous that the printed record should be not unworthy of its subject. It is fitting that the volume should forever be closely associated with Dr. Smyth, to whose memory it is affectionately dedicated. J. W. P.

ANDOVER, May 12, 1904.

[1] This message, with reply, is printed in Appendix II.

TABLE OF CONTENTS

	PAGE
PREFACE	5
PROGRAMME OF THE CELEBRATION	11
COMMEMORATIVE SERMON	13
The Rev. William Rogers Richards, D.D.	
INTRODUCTORY ADDRESS—Religious Conditions in New England in the time of Edwards	29
Professor John Winthrop Platner, D.D.	
ADDRESS—The Philosophy of Edwards	47
Professor Frederick J. E. Woodbridge, LL.D.	
ADDRESS—The Theology of Edwards	73
Professor Egbert Coffin Smyth, D.D., LL.D.	
POEM—A Witness to the Truth	95
President Samuel Valentine Cole, D.D.	
ADDRESS—The Influence of Edwards	105
Professor James Orr, D.D.	
APPENDICES	127

PROGRAMME

SUNDAY, OCT. 4
10.30 A. M.

PUBLIC WORSHIP in the Seminary Church.
> Sermon by the REV. WILLIAM ROGERS RICHARDS, D.D.
> New York

MONDAY, OCT. 5

AFTERNOON SESSION

3.30 O'CLOCK

PROFESSOR CHARLES ORRIN DAY, D.D., presiding.

DEVOTIONAL EXERCISES.

HYMN, No. 38. "All people that on earth do dwell."

WORDS OF WELCOME. . . PROFESSOR DAY

ADDRESS: Religious Conditions in New England in the Time of Edwards.
> PROFESSOR JOHN WINTHROP PLATNER, D.D.

ADDRESS: The Philosophy of Edwards.
> PROFESSOR FREDERICK J. E. WOODBRIDGE, LL.D.
> Columbia University

HYMN, No. 190. "Holy Spirit, Lord of Light." (5 stanzas)

RECEPTION AND COLLATION

BARTLET CHAPEL, 5.30 O'CLOCK

(For invited guests)

Exhibition of autograph and published writings of President Edwards and other objects of historical interest, loaned for the occasion.

EVENING SESSION

7.00 O'CLOCK

PROFESSOR EDWARD YOUNG HINCKS, D.D., presiding.

HYMN, No. 299. "Come, we who love the Lord."

PRAYER.

ADDRESS: The Theology of Edwards.
   PROFESSOR EGBERT COFFIN SMYTH, D.D., LL.D.

HYMN, No. 14. "Before Jehovah's awful throne."

POEM. - PRESIDENT SAMUEL VALENTINE COLE, D.D.
            Wheaton Seminary

CONGRATULATORY MESSAGE, from the Senate of the United Free Church College, Glasgow.

ADDRESS: The Influence of Edwards.
   PROFESSOR JAMES ORR, D.D., Glasgow.

HYMN, No. 663. "Let children hear the mighty deeds."

BENEDICTION.

SERMON

The Rev. WILLIAM ROGERS RICHARDS, D.D.

PASTOR OF

The Brick Presbyterian Church

NEW YORK CITY

SERMON

JEREMIAH 33: 17 — " For thus saith the Lord, David shall never want a man to sit upon the throne of the house of Israel."

The words are a prophecy of Christ and his eternal Kingdom, but the people who were first comforted by them had no clear expectation of that coming Kingdom. When they were told that David should never want a man, what they could first understand, — and no doubt did understand,— was this, that the breed of men of the old David-type was never to run out in Israel; that in every time of emergency and peril, when hearts were failing and knees trembling, — as in the old Philistine wars, when some Goliath was striding up and down between the camps insolently challenging any champion to appear for Israel,— in such dark days the right champion would appear; so the prophet says, the good cause would never be left to fall to the ground for lack of him. The Lord pledges his word to this. The thing is as sure as that covenant of the day and night which cannot fail while the world stands. And really that was the best promise that could be made to a people. For the gift of such a man as David was worth more to a nation than any other kind of gift that the Providence of God has ever bestowed. All the gold of India, and all the things that gold could buy, would not compare in value with this gift of a man.

What a poor little kingdom Israel was, judged by our common standards of wealth and power. There were richer nations on every side, better armed nations, more populous nations. But Israel had the man; no other of these nations, not all of them together, could show in those days a man like David, a man fit to sit on David's throne, a man with David's love for God, and trust in God, and earnest longing for God: and now those other nations, Babylon and Nineveh and Tyre and Egypt, with all their wealth and power, are mostly buried and forgotten as if they had never been; but David, this king of Israel! why, more people are singing his songs today, a hundred times over, than he ever ruled when he was alive. This influence is still increasing in the world. Such a man as that was the best gift that God could make to a nation. Now the promise was that so long as the nation of Israel continued, God would continue to bless them periodically with this gift of men. Of course there were some periods of great degeneracy when such men seemed very scarce, but the supply never quite ran out. Even in the worst times, when all things were falling into chaos, always just at the crisis would appear some Elijah, or John Baptist, or other like man, firm enough to stand, if need be, alone against the world, and pull the world his way, God's way. The man was never wanting in the old days in Israel.

And the man never shall be wanting. The

promise still stands in our Bible, only it has been freed from its old restriction to the nation of Israel. We have been taught to take all these promises more generously, but the promise has not been revoked. God is pledged to the world to keep up the breed of men. They may not always be Jews now; they may not always be Greeks, or Romans, or Englishmen, or even Americans; but there shall be such men; the race is not to run out. Whatever the pessimists may say, the final outcome of this great world-experiment is not to be the hopeless degeneracy of manhood. Today, tomorrow, next year, — so long as the old world stands, if ever old David should come back to it again, the promise is that he shall find somewhere the man fit to sit upon his throne. We may not always see this man, for we do not know where to look for him. In times of quiet when the world is moving on its way smoothly and easily, we may often doubt his existence; but when once more the storm breaks upon us, such times as try men's souls, there he stands, your Savonarola, Luther, Cromwell, Washington; all down through the ages, David has not lacked his man yet.

That is the promise; and, friends, how good a promise it is. For this manhood is God's most precious commodity: of all the things he has made this has cost the most to make, and is worth the most when made. We Christians always get some hint of the infinite costliness of manhood when we read in this book the price of our redemption, the precious blood of Jesus Christ. But even the older records of the rocks could tell a like story, for they show how lavishly the Creator has been using up whole races of his creatures in making way for man. If you are speaking of the expenditure of creative energy involved, I suppose a great mountain range is a very cheap product compared with one little child who is playing at the base of it. The whole land of Canaan had not cost so much in the making as that one man David.

And as this gift of manhood has cost more than all others, so it is worth more. Any great crisis proves it. Watch those tremendous forces of the French Revolution running out into horrible disaster, because, as Carlyle says, no Cromwell had appeared in France, no man able to control these forces. There were certain dark days in the earlier part of our own civil war, when, as someone has said, a man able to lead the army of the Potomac would have been worth to the national government in hard cash not less than a million dollars a day. For lack of such a leader the war was dragging on at that awful expenditure of wealth.

Our own age is one of great material progress, and there may be the more need to remind ourselves of this superlative value of manhood. Man's life consisteth not in the abundance of the things he possesseth, said the Master; but man is always in danger of thinking that it does consist in those things, when they are over-abundant. If he had little, — poor Peter, for instance, with his one little fishing boat, — he might make up his mind to throw that little away ; but the young ruler who had great possessions was in danger of throwing himself away instead. And so, in the bewildering abundance of good things which the Creator has now granted to have and enjoy, there is always danger that we men and women may lose a proper self-respect. We ought to remember that a nation might be enriched with all such gifts beyond the dreams of avarice, and yet not be worth a single day's visit from a man like David, if there was no hope of his finding in it a man to sit upon his throne.

We must remember this in connection with all the different departments of our national life.

When a foreigner comes to visit our country and asks what we have to show him worth seeing, many of us would point with peculiar pride to our schools and colleges, and that is well. But what if it should appear that what we really meant by a school was simply the fine building that houses it, or the many books in its library, or the costly apparatus in its laboratory, or the great size of its endowment ; the material things that it possesseth ? That would prove that we had not yet learned what a school really is. Money is not the school.

You will read of some great capitalist who has turned his pocket inside out and established a great university in our newer west ; an excellent thing for him to do. His gift creates an opportunity for the teacher, if only you can find the teacher; it sets up a throne, if only you can find the king. But that is all that money can do. All the wealth in Wall Street could not do for a college what Dr. Arnold did for Rugby; or what Longfellow and Lowell and Holmes, and the other members of that extraordinary literary circle, have done for Harvard; or what General Armstrong did for Hampton. The best promise possible for an institution of learning would not be that it shall never want money, but rather that it shall never want a man. We have never been told much about the endowments and buildings of the old Academy in Athens, or of the Lyceum; but the world will never forget the men — Plato and Aristotle. We do not hear of any endowments in that little college which grew up more than eighteen centuries ago by the shores of the Sea of Galilee; but the world will never forget the words that fell from the lips of its head Master, the Son of Man.

It is the man who makes the college, and on the other hand the one great work of the college ought to be the making of men. And I thank God for the old schools and colleges of New England, which, whatever their faults, have cherished faithfully the traditions of a worthy manhood.

So it is also in other departments of our national life, in the active professions, and in business. It might seem at first sight, that here the amount of capital was the essential thing, the quality of manhood only a secondary consideration; but it is not so. The life even of the business world consisteth not in the abundance of the things that it possesseth, but in the character of the men who are using the things. Given the right sort of men, and sooner or later there will be capital enough. But given the capital, you cannot be so sure that you will always find the right sort of men. The world has more capital now than it quite knows what to do with. Even at the low rate of four per cent., your savings bank sets a limit to the amount it is willing to receive from you. No lack of capital: it is waiting all about us for some one to use it. The lack is of the man who is strong enough to use it royally; and when once he appears, the man fit to sit on the throne of a great railroad corporation, or insurance company, or mining trust, and command it and make it go, — you know how such a man is prized, how much they will give him, — $10,000 a year, $25,000, $50,000. If he is man enough, he can almost name his own price.

It has been said lately that civilization is one long anxious search for the man who can carry a message to Garcia: and, we might add, for some other man who has a message worth sending to Garcia. The man is the great want in the business world.

And in the social life of every community, how we depend on the men and women of the royal type. It is they who make any society worth living in, and whose absence would make any society not worth living in. They make good society.

Money cannot make society, though it might easily destroy it. When the people had little, and lived near the natural realities; the backwoodsman with his ax and gun and paddle; the sailors who go down to the sea in ships and see the works of the Lord and his wonders in the deep; the farmer with his horses and cattle, and first-hand knowledge of the crops and how they fare in all sorts of weather — you know what good company such people are. Their range may be narrow, but within it they are perpetually interesting.

But give these same people what we call the advantages of wealth; let them shut themselves off from the real world by a multitude of man-made conventionalities and artifices; unless you are careful, you will find, as Tolstoi affirms with so much passion, that you have destroyed all their living human interest. The wealth that ought to have lifted and broadened them, has really cramped and stifled them; and all the usages of such a social world grow weary, stale, flat and unprofitable, till one might be tempted to repeat the remark of the witty French woman, that the more she saw of men the more highly she thought of dogs. That is what society often degenerates into. Oh, what need there is to remind ourselves in this age of the world that man's life consisteth not in the abundance of the things that he possesseth! The man himself is always what is wanted.

Now our text brings a promise from God that this perpetual want shall be perpetually supplied. If only you knew where to look for him, the man is somewhere to be found. If not in a palace up in Jerusalem, the Prince will be in a manger down in Bethlehem. God's promise shall not fail; David shall not want a man to sit upon the throne.

I have hoped that this old scripture text might be appropriate to the theme which will make tomorrow a memorable day here, and in so many of our older institutions of learning. In the New England of two hundred years ago God had his people, a peculiar people; and they found him still faithful to his promise, for among those early New Englanders there were never wanting men. From the very beginning the English Puritan movement had been distinguished for the honor it did to simple manhood. To a Puritan, rank and office and wealth, and all other outward accessories, sank into insignificance as compared with the human personality. Everyone knows Macaulay's description of those people, how they could look down with contempt on the great men of the earth in church and state, "being themselves noble by right of an earlier creation, and priests by the imposition of a mightier hand." These were the English Puritans. Now send off a ship-load of such people into any remote and desolate portion of the earth, and you may rest assured that they will be carrying with them, in the hull of their little ship, all the constituent elements of a great and prosperous commonwealth: for the reason that they themselves are men, and fit to sit on thrones.

Let me quote the words spoken last spring in the Congregational House in Boston, concerning the library there, with its treasure of old New England books. "For those who look upon these New England fields and hills," Dr. Gordon said, "as invested for more than two hundred years with the heroic humanity of their ancestors, who see the image of kingly men and queenly women burning in the sun that lights the world today, who hear in the murmur of the brook and the sigh of the river the voices that once made glad the holy places of the Most High, and who carry into the depth of nature, and into the contemporary world of man the sense of that pathetic, heroic, majestic past, these dead books will live again."

Yes, they were kingly men and queenly women, the writers of these books, and the other founders of New England; but among them all, or their descendants, there has not yet appeared a more kingly character than that great New Englander whose memory we shall celebrate tomorrow.

It is not for me at this service to attempt any analysis of Edwards's contributions to philosophy, or theology, or education, or the revival of the churches. Others fitter for the task will treat of these themes tomorrow. But I shall command your assent when I affirm that greater than all the wise things that

Jonathan Edwards may ever have said, and all the fine things that he may have done, was the man himself. What made that day two hundred years ago memorable was that then another man was born into the world. That was evident from the time when he began to resolve those strange youthful resolutions of his. Let me read you one or two of them : —

"Resolved so to live at all times, as I think is best in my devout frames, and when I have clearest notions of the Gospel and of another world."

Matthew Arnold was not the first to discover that

> "Tasks in hours of insight willed
> May be through hours of gloom fulfilled."

Again : "Resolved never to give over, nor in the least slacken my fight with my corruptions, however unsuccessful I may be."

Ah, another man had appeared!

And now after these long two hundred years, our American thought and life cannot escape the impress of that mighty personality. This celebration does not mean that all of us could profess ourselves his disciples in philosophy and theology. His teachings on the operations of human will, or of the divine justice, may seem to some of us quite as remote from our customary thought as the Ptolemaic system, or Plato's ideas. But we do all of us honor and celebrate the man. Whatever Edwards had to say, he spoke always with the royal accent : whatever he had to do, it was with the royal bearing. Watch him in the great crisis of his life, those days of bitterness and trial, when his people at Northampton turned against him, and drove him from the church and from the town; see his patience and magnanimity and courage. You see him every inch a king.

But had ever a great man a smaller stage for the display of his greatness? Through most of his life pastor of a little church in the country village of Northampton; then, for the few remaining years, a missionary at Stockbridge ministering to a few red sheep out there in the wilderness. To be sure he was called to the presidency of Princeton; but as if to prove that such a man as he owes nothing to the dignity of office, he died before he had fairly entered upon it. He had a son whom it may be proper to speak of as President Edwards. The father needs no such official title; Jonathan Edwards is his name, the man himself. It was a time of crisis, and the man was not wanting. God had kept his promise to his people. And so through all the celebrations of tomorrow we do well to cheer our hearts with the assurance that as it has been, so it shall be; and that to the end of the world, in the time of sorest need there shall never be wanting a man.

"Wanted a man." It is the great want always. A friend once asked me to preach a sermon on the theme, "Wanted a Saint." "Put it at your people," he said, "as an advertisement, as if it stood in the want-column in the newspaper, 'Wanted a Saint.'" It struck me as an attractive form of words; but when I tried to plan out the sermon, at once I ran up against a difficulty. Such advertisements in our papers, for coachmen, gardeners, cooks, and so forth, are designed to encourage applications from persons who deem themselves qualified to meet the want. But if you say "Wanted a Saint," and a stranger should then appear at your door and begin to rehearse his own saintly qualifications, you would feel like locking the stable and setting a guard on the hat-rack. The real saints are not so fluent about their own saintliness. You could not advertise for a saint, with any hope that the right person would apply.

But if not as an advertisement, you can issue this as a simple statement of the facts, "Wanted a Saint;" wanted a man of faith and character. Nothing else in this world is wanted so much; nothing else is worth so much. The community wants him; the Lord wants him: and the promise of our text is that this want, the world's great want, can always be supplied. By God's grace that very kind of manhood that is wanted from you or me may be had. The man who is wanted shall not be wanting, that is the promise. We must let the Lord fulfill that promise.

We are gathered here in a seat of learning, some of us in the immediate pursuit of an education. But the crown of education, the finest product of any school, is not the mere knowledge accumulated, it is the living personality developed; it is the man, the king, a man to sit upon the throne. Young Edwards, looking forward into the future, wrote down that long list of resolutions, and then spent his life in keeping them manfully. As we still look forward into the unknown future, any of us might well take example from him and ourselves subscribe a resolution; and we could not do better than borrow it from this ancient word of Sacred Writ: Whatever the unknown future may be, and wherever in it my lot may be ordered, I hereby resolve that, with God's help, "there shall not be wanting there a man to sit upon the throne."

Introductory Address

RELIGIOUS CONDITIONS IN NEW ENGLAND IN THE TIME OF EDWARDS

JOHN WINTHROP PLATNER, D.D.

Professor of History

Andover Theological Seminary

INTRODUCTORY ADDRESS

It falls to my lot, by way of introduction to the subject of the day, briefly to set before you the framework in which Edwards is the picture, to sketch the surroundings within which his life was passed, and in particular to describe the state of religion in New England in his time. To have value, this must be done with reference to the life and work of Edwards himself. Consequently I shall make little effort to examine conditions which are unrelated to this central figure, but shall rather fix your attention upon those with which he himself was intimately concerned, either by reason of their influence upon him, or, more important still, by reason of his influence upon them.

It is often asserted that all men, the great included, are the products of their age. The assertion contains no doubt a measure of truth. No man, however self-sufficient, can wholly shake off the influence of those political, social or religious conditions, in the midst of which he may chance to live. But to a certain number in every age it is given to bear the grave responsibility and enjoy the immeasurable opportunity of leadership, — to exemplify in their own persons not product, but process, — to set in order the forces which shall mould the course of history, — yes, to incarnate in themselves those very forces. Such men are in a true sense creative. And as we scrutinize their character, we discover there a quality, undefinable yet unmistakable, which we call detachment, — a certain independence of spirit and action, by virtue of which they rise superior to circumstance, superior to the common limitations of time and place, and take their station among the elect of all the ages. They are not wholly emancipated from their age, but they are released from bondage to it. They are no longer among the ruled, but among the rulers.

Jonathan Edwards illustrates, to a notable degree, this peculiar quality. He lived, and thought, and preached, and wrote in the New England of the eighteenth century, but in spirit he dwelt apart, where neither New England nor the eighteenth century controlled him, and from his isolation strove to gaze into the soul of things. To discern the constitution of the mind, to resolve the apparent antinomies of thought and experience, to justify the ways of God to man, even the most arbitrary, — these were his favorite employments. And in them all Edwards was spokesman for the race, though a still half-rude colony might be the theatre of his action, and the calendar mechanically register the dates of his mortal life. While he was grappling with the problem of the freedom of the will, far away across the sea another great philosopher, younger than himself, Immanuel Kant, was beginning to analyze the phenomena of consciousness, in search of its transcendental elements. How might each have elicited the other's best, if these two intellectual giants could have been brought face to face, and have held discourse concerning the fundamental realities! And how would Europe and America have stood in silent admiration at the matching of such wit as theirs! Kant was born, and lived, and died in Königsberg, on the eastern border of European civilization; Edwards dwelt in an English colony, on civilization's western frontier. But geography has never yet conquered genius, and provincial obscurity could not hide the spiritual light which streamed from these two great minds.

The career of Edwards, when judged by ordinary standards, would scarcely be called successful. His childhood indeed was full of brilliant promise; his student-life, most creditable; his brief term of service in a Yale tutorship, under circumstances of peculiar difficulty, an honor to himself and to his alma mater. His Northampton pastorate too, begun under the most favorable auspices, was carried on with earnestness and devotion, and accomplished marked results in arousing the indifferent to a new sense of the value of religion for human life. But with the lapse of time, Edwards encountered growing opposition, and his pastorate ended in sorrow for himself and dishonor for his parishioners. It seemed no doubt very like a professional failure when, at the age of forty-seven, he was dismissed from his charge and turned adrift upon the world.

He was not well adapted to meet the daily struggle for existence. Mere physical wants were never those which he was most interested in satisfying. Therefore we may well be thankful that, before too long a time had passed, the way was opened to another field of labor, where he could at least obtain the necessaries of life for his family and for himself. Patiently and cheerfully Edwards entered upon his new duties, with no word of rebuke for those who had rejected him, or of complaint against the lot which had brought him to so unpromising a field of labor. A true man of God, he won the hearts of the rude red men by his noble devotion, and brought into their lives a holy influence. Meanwhile he found intellectual satisfaction in creative labor, that most absorbing of occupations, and his thoughts lingered fondly in the most abstruse regions of metaphysical theology, where was their rightful home. But the settlement of the greatest philosopher of his day as a missionary among the Housatonic Indians, is again an event which must have seemed sadly to contravene the law of adaptation.

At last there came an opportunity which seemed better suited to a man of Edwards's powers, — the offer of the presidency of Princeton College. After long delay, and with manifest reluctance, he accepted and entered upon the duties of the office, but only to lay them down almost immediately at the stern bidding of death. This too, in the eyes of the world, would be counted a failure. Yet, standing at our vantage point of time, how different appears the verdict of history upon the whole of Edwards's career. Instead of failure we behold achievement of the highest order, we see forces set in operation which affected life at many points, stimulating thought, quickening conscience, reforming society, and creating — it is hardly too much to say — a new epoch for American Christianity.

Great political and religious changes had passed over the face of New England before Edwards came upon the scene. The original colonists had long been dead, and with them had vanished the early enthusiasm of their enterprise. Two generations had grown up under the hard conditions of frontier life, struggling with the reluctant northern soil, and constantly exposed to possible outbreaks of Indian ferocity. This contact with nature on her cruel side had rendered manners rude, and deadened spiritual sensibilities. Such education as Harvard was able to provide, although highly creditable to the colony, had not quite the same value as the university training the first settlers had enjoyed in their early English homes, and Yale College had but just opened its doors. At the beginning of the eighteenth century there were about one hundred and twenty churches of the Congregational order in New England, two-thirds of which were in Massachusetts. These embraced within their membership the large majority of professedly Christian people, yet the population was no longer religiously homogeneous. Not even the short and easy method of exclusion, formerly in vogue, had availed to preserve ecclesiastical purity. If non-conformists to "the New England way" had not succeeded in becoming permanent residents of the colonies, they at least had managed occasionally to stay long enough to start their propaganda, and always long enough to arouse dissension.

Baptists had vexed the souls of the dominant party ever since John Clarke began to minister in Newport, and since Roger Williams and his twelve companions were "plunged" in Providence. The defection of President Dunster had alarmed all those interested in Harvard College, and moved the Cambridge minister to preach "more than half a score of ungainsayable sermons" in defence of "the comfortable truth" of infant baptism. As the seventeenth century progressed, the leaders of the theocracy took vigorous measures to suppress the objectionable sect. "Experience tells us," says Samuel Willard, "that such a rough thing as a New England Anabaptist is not to be handled over-tenderly." Yet the Baptists increased and, in Edwards's time, they formed an important element of the population.

It may seem strange that the Religious Society of Friends should ever have been a disturbing element in any Christian community, yet so it was. When the "truth," as taught by George Fox and his followers, "brake forth in America," like many another truth in the course of history, it was unrecognized, spurned, and tried in the fires of persecution, that its alloy of error might be removed. The time had not yet come when the colonists would recognize the truth, — which seems now as elementary as it is Biblical, — that "the manifestation of the spirit is given to every man to profit withal." That time, however, would come, and all the sooner for the mysticism of Edwards, which after all is not remotely akin to that of Fox.

By far the most disliked and distrusted of all religious bodies in New England, next to the "Scarlet Woman" herself, was the Episcopal church. In the year of Edwards's birth, Keith and Talbot were touring the colonies in the interest of the Society for the Propagation of the Gospel. Just after Edwards's graduation, Yale College, which was relied upon to preserve genuine Puritan traditions, along with its cultivation of sound learning, threatened to apostatize, losing Rector Cutler and a tutor to the Episcopal communion. Not a little of the labor and responsibility required to maintain order and restore confidence in the college at this crisis, rested upon the shoulders of Edwards, and worthily did he repay the confidence reposed in him. He took no active part, it is true, in open warfare against the Anglicans, but the principles of his teaching were such as to give stability and strength to the churches of his own order. One finds, however, that anxiety over the gains made by Anglicanism throughout New England, and over proposals to procure an American episcopate, continued far beyond the limits of Edwards's life-time. Among the "trials and difficulties," of which the Diary of Ezra Stiles gives a formidable list, we find " concern for the Congregational churches, and the prevalence of episcopacy and wickedness."

The new charter of the Bay colony, issued the year Timothy Edwards was graduated from Harvard, greatly altered the political situation by widening the suffrage and substituting what must have seemed like a secularized commonwealth in place of the old theocracy. Joshua Scottow's pathetic book, entitled "Old Men's Tears," bears witness to the feeling of despondency felt by conservative men, as they beheld the passing of the old order. The year before Edwards was born, in the procession in Boston held in honor of the proclamation of Queen Anne, the ministers no longer took precedence of the civil magistrates.

The change which was perhaps most keenly felt was the abolition of the special privileges long enjoyed by adherents of the " standing order." What the national church was to England, that Congregationalism has been to the colony of Massachusetts Bay. The principle of toleration was new. It had but lately and reluctantly been recognized in the mother country, and it had many foes both there and in America. Increase Mather said of it, " I do believe that antichrist hath not in this day a more probable way to advance the kingdom of darkness." This principle, which permitted the existence, and thereby encouraged the growth of several ecclesiastical bodies, was destined greatly to alter the religious complexion of New England. Edwards lived at the time when denominational history was just beginning. Now throughout the protestant world denominationalism has been largely determined by doctrinal divergences. This was the case in the eighteenth century, both in England and in America, and to Edwards more than to anyone else, — far more than to his great contemporary, John Wesley, — belongs the responsibility of having sharply defined the theological differences of that formative period.

Christian life at the opening of the eighteenth century was probably less decadent in the American colonies than in England, where the corrupt social heritage of the Restoration, the popularity of a superficial "natural religion," and the irreligious influence of the French school were largely responsible for the condition of affairs. Orthodox belief and moral conduct had seemed there to degenerate together. A coarse cynicism characterized the speech and action of many of the gentry, and it was jestingly proposed that Parliament should pass an act omitting the word "not" from the Decalogue and inserting it in the Creed. But if moral deterioration in New England was less marked, it was nevertheless grave enough, and the very severe codes of law then in force seemed unable to check its progress. Religious indifference was correspondingly wide-spread.

Then, at the time of greatest need, the cause of vital religion in old England, thanks to the Wesleyan movement, received a fresh influx of splendid energy, which permeated all classes of society, and turned back the tide of irreligion and moral laxity. In New England, at the same time, the "Great Awakening," as it must ever be called, infused new life into every church and community within her borders. And it was Jonathan Edwards more than anyone else, — with the sincerity, earnestness and directness of his preaching, — who started this vast movement. The Awakening was far from being merely a series of sensational revivals. In spite of its fanatical excesses (with which Edwards had no sympathy), it was accompanied by a veritable moral reformation. Edwards directed all his preaching, even the most terrible, towards the great end of transforming character in accordance with the will of God. How he harmonized his theological determinism with his proclamation of the Gospel, his realistic portraitures of future woe with his doctrine of the divine love, we need not here inquire. The problems are at least as old as St. Paul. And just such antinomies as these, although incapable of solution by the laws of logic, are proved historically to be no bar to useful and effective service in the kingdom of Christ.

Edwards found New England morally decadent; he left it under the power of an awakened moral sense. But this result was wrought by distinctively religious means. Edwards made no effort to be a moral reformer without morality's highest sanction, and against the Arminian conception of virtue he registered an unqualified protest. No human effort, no ethical teaching, however lofty, could avail to change the heart or transform character. Only divine power could do this, working from within outward, making the tree good from its roots, cleansing the heart, out of which are the issues of life. And the moral tonic thus administered accomplished its cure. "Conversion" did result in moral reformation. By means of his accurate insight into the nature of true virtue, Edwards established anew the rightful relationship between cause and effect in character-building. But if he denied the efficacy of unaided human effort to save the soul, he also denied the efficacy of a mere correct religious theory. "No merely speculative understanding of the doctrines of religion" would suffice. Only the power of God, with its response in the life of obedient faith, could perform the miracle.

Edwards found ecclesiastical discipline relaxed under the system of the half-way covenant; he overthrew that system, tightened the cords which bound believers into one body, and redeemed the churches from secularization. The half-way covenant had long been in use in Northampton and in other sections of New England, where it had come to enjoy all the prestige of established custom. It is a shallow optimism which would regard this phenomenon as insignificant. A vital issue was at stake, namely this: is religion form, or is it substance? If candidates were admitted to the church without manifesting any fitness to assume its responsibilities, the church would at once take on the character of a *corpus permixtum*, a character which, however true or false in itself, was clearly in violation of the historic principles of Puritanism. Edwards combatted this conception, and it cost him his pastorate; but the qualifications for full communion were once more stated, in their earlier sense, and sooner or later the churches came over to his view.

Edwards found New England un-theological; he left it equipped with all the apparatus for an energetic theological life. When he began his ministry the churches lacked a just appreciation of the value of Christian theology, and of the beneficial service it should be made to render. To be sure, the early colonists had brought with them the system of doctrine generally accepted by English Puritans, and the Westminster standards had always been those of American Congregationalism. But orthodoxy, in Edwards's day, had become stereotyped and conventional. The familiar history of all scholasticism was here being repeated, the end of which is death. No great leaders had arisen to state anew the problems of theology, much less to attempt their solution. But upon these problems Edwards pondered long and deeply. He noted, in his own experience, divergences from those conventional rules which he had been taught were universal. And when he discovered that he had not "experienced regeneration exactly in those steps in which divines say it is generally wrought," he resolved "never to leave searching" until he had discovered "why they used to be converted in those steps."

Now this is the first step in theological progress, boldly to confront and to interrogate the past. Always respectful toward his predecessors, Edwards was not the blind follower of any, and his independence, and effort to be thorough, while they led him into no heresies, as they have led some others, did lead him so to restate the doctrines commonly called Calvinistic, as to open a new chapter of American religious thought.

Theological parties are rightly described as dating from this time, and it was Edwards's sharp definition of the issues which called them into being. He himself stands at the head of that highly interesting succession of divines, — Hopkins, Bellamy, Emmons, Dwight and the rest, down to our own Professor Park, — who are known as the "New England School." Recoiling from the severity of his clear-cut Calvinism, the Arminian party diverged from the Edwardean, and sub-divided within itself. The more evangelical wing, under the leadership of Wesley and his followers, moved on into Methodism, now numerically the strongest protestant communion in the world.

The less evangelical, under the leadership of Chauncy, Mayhew, and later James Freeman, developed into the liberal societies called Unitarian, now numerically among the weakest. Of other varieties of theological opinion, many of which find their beginning in this formative period, there is no time to speak.

But when we ask ourselves what service Edwards rendered which appeals most strongly to the religious sympathies of today, I think we shall not find it in his system of theology. We must rather seek it in his spiritual insight and his mysticism. He had beheld not simply the infernal terrors but also the beatific vision, and this was for him evermore the profoundest of realities. Direct intuition of God's will and personal communion with the Holy Spirit were the forces which controlled him. His purely *religious* influence, stamped clear and strong upon his own age, is one of the church's most precious possessions. Systems of thought may arise, and flourish, and decay; though they bear within them the potency of life, yet it is in ever changing forms, and the fact of their continuity may easily escape all but professional students of the past. In the great circuit of the world's intelligence, they have no continuing city. But the search of a soul after God stands possessed of an imperishable interest. Whether it be an Origen or an Augustine, a St. Francis or a Luther, a Wesley or an Edwards, ancient and modern times unite in paying homage to their memory. And upon the face of the fair monuments which posterity shall rear, this inscription should ever stand: Here once more, in the person of this man of God, was exemplified the union of the human and the divine. As the flower turns upward, to drink in the sun's life-giving beams, so this soul opened towards heaven, and received the very life of God.

Address

THE PHILOSOPHY OF EDWARDS

FREDERICK J. E. WOODBRIDGE, LL.D.

Professor of Philosophy

Columbia University

THE PHILOSOPHY OF EDWARDS

In the preface to his book on Jonathan Edwards, Professor Allen quotes with approval the remark of Bancroft, "He that would know the workings of the New England mind in the middle of the last century, and the throbbings of its heart, must give his days and nights to the study of Jonathan Edwards." And Professor Allen adds, "He that would understand the significance of later New England thought, must make Edwards the first object of his study." Time has at last set the limit to the truth of such remarks. To understand the philosophy and theology of today in New England or the country at large, the student must undoubtedly seek his foundations elsewhere than in the thought of Edwards. His influence is now largely negligible. The type of thinking which most widely prevails, is so far removed from him, in such notable contrast to him, finds its roots so markedly in other sources, that interest in him is more antiquarian than vitalizing. But the remarkable thing is that these statements, true today, were not true in 1889, when Professor Allen's book appeared. To question then the soundness of his estimate, or that of Bancroft's, could at best involve only the censure of a mild exaggeration. A few days and nights, even at that time, might have been spared the student of New England thought from surrender to Edwards.

That less than twenty years could have involved

such a change, is itself a significant commentary on the power of Edwards's work. It has failed not through refutation, but through inadequacy. Today we get so much more elsewhere, and find other richer sources to stir us to progress or controversy. It is to Greek philosophy, and to British and German philosophy and theology, that the student must give his days and nights, if he is to understand our thought. And so for us, I take it, New England thought, impressed in its beginnings so potently by Edwards that he dominated it either positively or negatively for a century and a half, has failed to afford a foundation for progressive development in either philosophy or theology. It is to be noted further that the foundations we now rest upon, have not been laid by our contemporaries. They reach far back into the past, to Edwards's contemporaries abroad, to his predecessors by many centuries. Significant as the thought of New England has been on its speculative side, it has not contained enough native, original strength to preserve it from the inadequacy which profoundly marked it through its ignorance of history. The courses in philosophy and theology offered in our colleges, universities, and seminaries today, are so immeasurably superior to those offered twenty years ago, that one can readily understand why the types of philosophy and theology are so vastly different and owe such different allegiance. But one would be a poor observer, if he did not recognize the peculiar vigor of that

New England thought, which may have ceased to influence him profoundly.

So I would not have these remarks construed into a belittling of Edwards or his influence. I have made them because, in connection with that influence, they indicate the fact from which it must be estimated. More than this: this fact, viewed in the light of what Edwards himself did and of what his early years gave promise, has given me the most suggestive insight into the man's power and versatility, and a more satisfactory estimate of his personality as a thinker. For he was a man with an undeveloped possibility, greater to my mind than the actuality attained. He did not belong to the men we cannot imagine different, but to the men, whom, the better we know them, the more we seem compelled to view in other light. What he might have been, becomes, at least for the student of philosophy, as insistent and suggestive a question as what he was.

One cannot write history as it ought to have been. Yet this truth ought not to blind us to the fact that there have been great persons, whose position in history has been not only influential, but, more significantly, critical. To such persons is chargeable not only what their influence has been, but also what it has not been. If the thought of New England has been largely determined by Edwards in its positive achievements, it has been almost equally determined by him in what it has failed to achieve, for he undoubtedly possessed, although he did not carry through in his work, those elements which in large measure would have made that thought more stable and lasting. It has failed through lack of real philosophical insight. But it was just this insight which Edwards possessed in a very remarkable degree, but failed to carry through in his work. And this is the more significant because no other American, perhaps, has possessed philosophical insight of equal power.

It would of course be futile to attempt to say what American thought would have been if Edwards had not lacked philosophical thoroughness. Yet it appears to me undoubtedly true that it no longer finds him influential because of just this lack, and that it presents today little continuity with its past. It has appeared to me instructive, therefore, to consider with some detail, this lack of philosophical thoroughness in Edwards's work, in order to an appreciation of his critical significance in the history of American thinking, and of the profoundly interesting character of his own thought.

Edwards's "Notes on the Mind," of uncertain though doubtless early date, incomplete, detached, and of most varying worth, are doubtless for the student of philosophy the most impressive products of Edwards's thought. While they reveal his philosophical ability as perhaps none of his publications reveals it, they cannot be credited with contributing to his influence. They were not a known factor.

They are not inconsistent with his elaborate treatises, as Professor Gardiner maintains that they are not, but one would not be led to suspect them from these treatises. I dismiss consideration of them for the present, therefore, to return to them after speaking of some of his completed works. Foremost of these is undoubtedly his "Enquiry into Freedom of Will."

The reader of this Enquiry today must add his tribute to the many bestowed by others on its greatness. But just because it is so great, its lack of philosophical thoroughness is remarkable. What amazes one about it is that an analysis of the will so acute, so sane, so dispassionate, so free from prejudice or tricky argument, and so sound, if the distinction of terms made by Edwards is admitted, could yet, with hardly a trace of rational justification, be linked with a Calvinistic conception of God and the world. I do not mean that it is at all amazing that Edwards's conception of the will should be held by Calvinists, or be thought consistent with their positions, but rather that a mind that could so profoundly philosophize about the will, could be so insensible of the need of further philosophy to link his results with his theological convictions. More than this: that a mind so fair and dispassionate in his analysis of the will, could be so unfair and passionate in his theological setting of it.

The first two parts of the Enquiry, with the exception of Sections 11 and 12 of Part II, which are exegetical, are to be classed among the greatest of philosophical writings. That Edwards is not unique in what he here discloses does not detract from his greatness. Spinoza, Hobbes and Hume all have the same doctrine, but exhibit no greater philosophical skill in the exposition of it. Significant too for his remarkable power is the fact that these men had, at first hand, acquaintance with other philosophies, which he altogether lacked. In these parts, and indeed in the whole work, wherever Edwards seeks to fix or distinguish terms, he is remarkably acute. A notable illustration of this among many equally notable, is his analysis of the term "action" in Part IV, Section 2. His clear insistence on the need of such analysis, and his skill in executing it, rank him among the great logicians. Simple distinctions in argument, but of weighty import, abound, such as this: "Infallible foreknowledge may prove the necessity of the event foreknown, and yet not be the thing which causes the necessity." Everywhere the impression is left that such simple distinctions are the fruit of careful thought and the utterances of a mind sure of its grasp. So long as Edwards gives himself up to the analysis, this sureness is evident, so evident indeed, that he lets the argument carry itself by its own worth without any attempt at persuasion.

The results of the analysis are notable. Necessity may be one in philosophical definition, but it is as diverse in existence as the realms where it is found.

Natural and moral necessity are both necessity, but different kinds of it. Causal relations may exist between mental events as well as between physical events, without making mental events physical. What makes moral necessity repugnant is its confusion with natural necessity, which is as if one were to confuse mind with matter. We should recognize too that necessity is not some exterior fate, compelling events, but the actual linkage which the events disclose in their existence, and that they do disclose such linkage wherever they exist, in the mind as well as in nature. Did it not exist in the mind, there would then be no linkage between motive and act, between end and means. Again, whether an act is voluntary, and so free, depends on whether it is the result of volition or of something else. The causes of volition, whatever they may be, do not affect its voluntary aspect or destroy the function of the will, any more than the causes of life destroy the functions of life. Again, moral praise or blame does not belong to the causes of men's acts but to the acts themselves, just as natural praise or blame belongs not to the causes of a thing but to its value. Yet moral merit is different from natural merit, as the mind is different from nature. So one might continue until he had exhibited all the results of the analysis.

I am of course aware that attempts have been made to overthrow this analysis of Edwards, but I confess that I find nothing in the analysis which should lead one to make the attempt. Motives to that effort are derived from other sources, and almost exclusively from ethical or theological interests. Nothing in the whole analysis is hostile to morality, until that analysis ceases to be analysis, and becomes instead a revelation of God's activity or the secret workings of some ultimate being. It is not hostile to morality because it discloses most powerfully and convincingly the fact that man by the necessity of his own nature must act and judge with an appreciation of the value and responsibility of his acts, just as the sun by the necessity of its own nature must shine. To show that is not to drive morality out of human life, but to found it in the constitution of things. It is philosophy at its best.

And just because it is philosophy at its best, we look eagerly for its continuance. But here Edwards fails us. He does not continue. Perhaps he could not. And the fact that he did not, or could not, is the critical thing for his philosophy and influence. As we proceed to the remaining parts of the Enquiry, containing his polemic against the Arminians, we pursue arguments which have no philosophical relation to what has preceded. There is no longer philosophical analysis and construction at a sustained height, but only flashes of it here and there, amid pages of rhetorical attempts at persuasion, tricky arguments, and sophistry. There is no philosophical carrying through of the doctrine of the will. Repeatedly he is content to dispose of a difficulty in Calvinism by pointing out that Arminianism has the same difficulty. He argues that if total moral inability excuses a man totally, partial inability should excuse him partially, and in proper numerical proportion. This remarkable argument he illustrates by his figure of the balance which can turn ten pounds but no more, forgetting, apparently, the deep significance of the fact that it *can* turn anything less than ten pounds, forgetting, in short, the vast difference between degrees of ability and no ability at all. To the objection that men are blameless if God gives them up to sin, he can only cry, "Then Judas was blameless after Christ had given him over." To these instances of philosophical weakness many more could be added, especially Part IV, Section 9, where the question is discussed, "How God is concerned in the existence of sin." It is exceptionally remarkable that the man who wrote the first two parts of the work could have written this section. His apparent unconsciousness of the significance of the fact that his own theory of the will might, with equal justice, be linked with totally different ultimate positions, is also noteworthy. He recognizes the simple and cogent truth that his doctrine is not false just because Hobbes and the Stoics held it. But he fails to see that their holding of it may point to other conclusions than the Calvinistic.

It is not that Edwards prostitutes his philosophy

to his theological convictions. To my mind there is not the slightest proof of that, and, so far as I know, it has never been seriously maintained. The fact is rather that the philosopher never became the theologian or the theologian the philosopher. It is futile to try to understand Edwards's Calvinism from his philosophy or his philosophy from his Calvinism. In him they are juxtaposed, not united. But they are not equally juxtaposed. The theology overshadows the philosophy. The latter, however, is of such superior merit to the former in depth of insight and cogency of reasoning, that one is irresistibly led to speculate on what Edwards would have been, if the philosophy had overshadowed the theology. One recognizes that his influence would have been vastly different, that it has consequently been a critical influence for American thought.

This juxtaposition instead of union of philosophy and theology is seen in Edwards's other work. I will consider it in the two remaining writings which are of particular philosophical interest, namely the dissertations on "God's Last End in the Creation," and the "Nature of True Virtue." These dissertations, although never published by Edwards, were written earlier than his last publication in 1757. They are not, even if actually written after the "Enquiry Concerning Freedom of Will," unpremeditated works. The suggestion of them is frequent in his sermons and other writings, from which we could largely construct them. One naturally asks, therefore, why they were not published. Unpublished manuscripts left by eminent men is so frequent an occurrence, that the question might be answered by this common fact. But acquaintance with those dissertations gives a pointed interest to the question. For while they present a general agreement with the rest of Edwards's work, and evince that juxtaposition of philosophy and theology which has been remarked, they exhibit a real simplification of his thought and suggestive indications of almost conscious attempts at unification. Their total effect is rather to weaken than to strengthen his theology. As they are not essentially polemic, but rather more the work of a disinterested inquirer, the logical trend of the thought becomes more natural and inevitable. All the more logical revulsion is occasioned consequently by the juxtaposition of the elements of an unrelated theology. One is led to suspect that Edwards was becoming conscious of his intellectual duality, and that the dissertations were not published because they must consequently appear to him as incomplete, as faulty, as demanding the work of adjustment. His original power, his versatility, his constant growth, make it improbable that his death in his fifty-fifth year occurred when his intellectual life was fixed beyond alteration. One is tempted, therefore, to regard these later writings, not as the mere conclusions of previous positions, but as works of promise.

It is interesting to note that the dissertation on

"God's Last End in the Creation" begins, after an explanation of terms, with a consideration of "what reason dictates in this affair," although it is admitted that the affair is "properly an affair of divine revelation." The justification of reason's dictates in spite of this fact, really amounts to submitting the facts of revelation to the judgment of reason. For Edwards contends that "no notion of God's last end in the creation of the world is agreeable to reason, which would truly imply any indigence, insufficiency, and mutability in God." This dictate of reason, with which, as Edwards would show, revelation is in most consistent agreeableness, contains in undeveloped form the recognition of God's last end in the creation. God is his own last end. The developed form of this statement we read, wondering if indeed these are the words of the greatest of American theologians, and not rather the words of some disciple of Plotinus or of a Christian Spinoza. "As there is an infinite fulness of all possible good in God — a fulness of every perfection, of all excellency and beauty, and of infinite happiness — and as this fulness is capable of communication, or emanation *ad extra;* so it seems a thing amiable and valuable in *itself* that this infinite fountain of good should send forth abundant streams. And as this is in itself excellent, so a *disposition* to this in the divine being, must be looked upon as an *excellent* disposition. Such an emanation of good is, in some sense, a *multiplication* of it. So far as the stream may be looked upon as anything besides the fountain, so far it may be looked on as an *increase* of good. And if the fulness of good that is in the fountain, is in itself excellent, then the emanation, which is as it were an increase, repetition, or multiplication of it, is excellent. Thus it is fit, since there is an infinite fountain of light and knowledge, that this light should shine forth in beams of communicated knowledge and understanding: and as there is an infinite fountain of holiness, moral excellence and beauty, that so it should flow out in communicated holiness. And that, as there is an infinite fulness of joy and happiness, so these should have an emanation, and become a fountain flowing out in abundant streams, as beams from the sun. Thus it appears reasonable to suppose that it was God's last end, that there might be a glorious and abundant emanation of his infinite fulness of good *ad extra*, or without himself; and that the disposition to communicate himself, or diffuse his own FULNESS, was what moved him to create the world." Mystic pantheism could not be more explicit.

Edwards appears not to have been wholly insensible to the possibility of such an interpretation. And here is to be noted an instance of that apparent consciousness of a need of unification which has been remarked. The first objection against his view which he considers is to the effect that his position may be "inconsistent with God's absolute independence and immutability: particularly, as though God were inclined to a communication of his fulness, and emanations of his own glory, as being his own most glorious and complete state." To this he answers, "Many have wrong notions of God's happiness, as resulting from his absolute self-sufficience, independence and immutability. Though it be true, that God's glory and happiness are in and of himself, are infinite and cannot be added to, and unchangeable, for the whole and every part of which he is independent of the creature; yet it does not hence follow, nor is it true, that God has no real and proper delight, pleasure or happiness, in any of his acts or communications relative to the creature, or effects he produces in them; or in anything he sees in his creatures' qualifications, dispositions, actions and state. God may have a real and proper pleasure or happiness in seeing the happy state of the creature; yet this may not be different from his delight in himself." To let this answer suffice, reason must silence its questions. It is no answer at all, but simply a theological proposition juxtaposed to the philosophy.

The silencing of reason is still more apparent in his second answer to the objection. "If any are not satisfied with the preceding answer, but still insist on the objection, let them consider whether they can devise any other scheme of God's last end in creating the world, but what will be equally obnoxious to this objection in its full force, if there be any force in it."

Surely we have in this dissertation no thorough consideration of what reason dictates in the affair. He has in effect, as Professor Allen justly remarks, "sacrificed all that is not God," and all the theology of the world superimposed and insisted on, cannot avoid that sacrifice. The mind that produced the work on the will, and had so irresistibly followed the dictates of reason up to this point, may have been unconscious of the gap. If so, this unconsciousness reveals anew the sharp duality in this great intellect. If not, adjustment of some sort must have been felt to be necessary, before the work could be given to the world.

If the Calvinistic theology it contains should be eliminated from the dissertation on the "Nature of True Virtue," there would remain a conception of virtue almost identical with Spinoza's. Disinterested love to God is presented as the highest exercise of the virtuous man, who will exercise it highly in proportion to his knowledge of God, and also will desire that as many as possible should share in the same exercise and enjoy its benefits. These benefits do not really consist in rewards, but the virtuous soul finds in virtue itself its true good and highest happiness. "So far as the virtuous mind exercises true virtue in *benevolence* to created beings, it seeks chiefly the good of the creature; consisting in its *knowledge* or view of God's glory and beauty, its *union* with God, conformity and love to him, and joy in him."

This is all in thorough harmony with Spinoza.

But Edwards's total conception differs from Spinoza's in one very important particular. With Spinoza man must love God in proportion as he knows God, and ignorance of the divine nature is consequently the cause of all wickedness, is indeed wickedness itself. But with Edwards man may know God completely and yet remain vicious. The devils believe and tremble, but cease not, therefore, to be devils. For while virtue grows as the knowledge of God grows, a virtuous disposition must first be given, natural or derived. Without such a virtuous disposition implanted or native in the heart, there can be no virtuous exercise. Wherever in intelligent beings this disposition is lacking, vice must prevail in spite of perfect knowledge of God and his last end in the creation. "Christians," says Edwards, "have the greatest reason to believe, from the scriptures, that in the future day of the revelation of the righteous judgment of God, when sinners shall be called to answer before their judge, and all their wickedness, in all its aggravations, brought forth and clearly manifested in the perfect light of that day; and God shall reprove them, and set their sins in order before them, their consciences will be greatly awakened and convinced, their mouths will be stopped, all stupidity of conscience will be at an end, and conscience will have its full exercise; and therefore their consciences will *approve* the dreadful sentence of the judge against them; and seeing that they deserved so great a punishment, will join with the judge in condemning them. . . . . Then the sin and wickedness of their heart will come to its highest dominion and completest exercise; they shall be wholly left of God, and given up to their wickedness, even as the devils are! When God has done waiting on sinners, and his Spirit done striving with them, he will not restrain their wickedness as he does now. But sin shall then rage in their hearts, as a fire no longer restrained and kept under."

This emphasis on the necessity of a virtuous disposition to the exercise of virtue, was one of the important principles in Edwards's doctrine of the will. Its reappearance here is natural. But it reappears with such force and clearness as to amount to the recognition of something arbitrary in the scheme of things, an element persistently refusing to be related, a reality naturally and originally obnoxious to God. It seriously interferes with the divine power. It can have no place in a world which is the emanation of the divine fulness of perfection. One is tempted to think that its presence in Edwards's thinking is due to a concession to his theology, that it is another instance of that unrelated juxtaposition I have insisted on. And so it may well be. But it serves to make that juxtaposition still more apparent. It is true, however, that this dissertation on the nature of true virtue, if taken by itself, exhibits a greater degree of philosophical thoroughness than is to be found elsewhere in Edwards's work. Whatever may have influenced him thus to emphasize the underlying necessity of a virtuous disposition to the exercise of virtue, this dissertation, with the principle admitted, is most thoroughly worked out. And it is just this thoroughness which makes the dissertation emphasize anew the duality of Edwards's mind. It emphasizes it so emphatically, that the suspicion is once more aroused that he was beginning to feel the need of adjustment between the unrelated elements of his thought.

Lack of adjustment, the juxtaposition of unrelated principles in an ordinary mind, is not a cause of interest. But I have tried to point out that in Edwards there is no ordinary juxtaposition. It is extraordinary. It is crucial for our understanding of the man. It is necessary for a clear characterization of his influence. It reveals itself with such steady accumulation as to amount to a demand, not altogether conscious perhaps, for a revision of the whole system. It reveals Edwards not as a man of a single idea, with opinions changelessly fixed and doggedly supported, but as a man of remarkable versatility, of steady growth, of rich promise, but as a man too, who only late in life gave evidence of a possible unification of the diverse elements of his nature. Of these elements the theological was the most prominent both by his exposition and his personal influence. It was his theology that he bequeathed to New England, his theology, be it said, however, stamped with the peculiar force of his great personality. And it was not a philosophically grounded theology. Its own force spent, it could not draw on Edwards's other work. Its failure of continued influence becomes his failure. Yet philosophy was there with unusual excellence. Surely one must recognize that Edwards has influenced American thought critically, that he gave to it, in its first significant and original outburst, the theological instead of the philosophical cast, with a theology left so unrelated to a real insight into human nature and the world's nature, that it was bound to fail with the failure of personal conviction of its truth.

A man so profoundly interesting on account of his versatility and the peculiar way its elements were composed in him, so interesting too on account of the nature of his influence, cannot be dismissed without some attempt at an understanding of his intellectual character. It is too easy an explanation of him which would point to his time, his education, his occupation. For, let me insist again, he was distinctly a great man. He did not merely express the thoughts of his time, or meet it simply in the spirit of his traditions. He stemmed it and moulded it. New England thought was already making toward that colorless theology which marked it later. That he checked. It was decidedly Arminian. He made it Calvinistic. To his own personal convictions he was forced, through his removal from Northampton, to sacrifice the work in which he had unselfishly spent his best years. His time does not explain him. We must look to his intellectual history.

Perhaps he would remain altogether enigmatic, were it not for what he has told us of himself, and for what his early "Notes on the Mind" reveal. These Notes contain an outline of philosophy, which for penetration and breadth of interest finds no superior in the work of other minds equally mature. More than this, it surpasses the work of many maturer minds which have yet received the recognition of history. We know that its inspiration was mainly Locke, but its promise of superiority to him is evident. The remarkable verbal similarity these Notes reveal to the writings of Berkeley, has led to a comparison of Edwards with the Irish bishop and a search for traces of his influence. These have not been found. Nor is the philosophy unmistakably Berkeley's. It is more the germ of that mystic pantheism which was disclosed later with such clearness in the dissertation on God's Last End in the Creation. The trend of his thinking is not so much revealed in such Berkeleyan expressions as these: "When we say that the World, i. e. the material Universe exists nowhere but in the mind, we have got to such a degree of strictness and abstraction, that we must be exceedingly careful, that we do not confound and lose ourselves by misapprehension. That is impossible, that it should be meant, that all the world is contained in the narrow compass of a few inches of space, in little ideas in the place of the brain; for that would be a contradiction; for we are to remember that the human body, and the brain itself, exist only mentally, in the same sense that other things do; and so that, which we call *place*, is an idea too. Therefore things are truly in those places; for what we mean, when we say so, is only, that this mode of our idea of place appertains to such an idea. We would not therefore be understood to deny, that things are where they seem to be. For the principles we lay down, if they are narrowly looked into, do not infer that. Nor will it be found, that they at all make void Natural Philosophy, or the science of the Causes or Reasons of corporeal changes. For to find out the reasons of things, in Natural Philosophy, is only to find out the proportion of God's acting. And the cause is the same, as to such proportions, whether we suppose the World only mental, in our sense, or no."

The trend of his thinking is revealed rather in such pantheistic expressions as these: "Seeing God has so plainly revealed himself to us; and other minds are made in his image, and are emanations from him; we may judge what is the Excellence of other minds, by what is his, which we have shown is Love. His Infinite Beauty is his Infinite mutual Love of Himself. Now God is the Prime and Original Being, the First and Last, and the Pattern of all, and has the sum total of all perfection. We may therefore, doubtless, conclude, that all that is the perfection of Spirits may be resolved into that which is God's perfection, which is Love." "When we speak of Being in general, we may be understood of the Divine Being, for he is an Infinite Being : therefore all others must necessarily be considered as nothing. As to *Bodies*, we have shown in another place, that they have no proper Being of their own. And as to *Spirits*, they are the communications of the Great Original Spirit ; and doubtless, in metaphysical strictness and propriety, He is, as there is none else. He is likewise Infinitely Excellent, and all Excellence and Beauty is derived from him, in the same manner as all Being. And all other Excellence, is, in strictness only a shadow of his." " We shall be in danger, when we meditate on this love of God to himself, as being the thing wherein his infinite excellence and loveliness consists, of some alloy to the sweetness of our view, by its appearing with something of the aspect and cast of what we call self-love. But we are to consider that this love includes in it, or rather is the same as, a love to everything, as they are all communications of himself. So that we are to conceive of Divine Excellence as the Infinite General Love, that which reaches all, proportionally, with perfect purity and sweetness."

Indeed if these Notes inspire one to curious research into the indebtedness of Edwards to others, Berkeley is but one of several philosophers that will be suggested. But the search thus far has been vain, and it appears true that its vanity is due, not to the lack of evidence, but to the fact that there is no indebtedness which can be counted as significant. These Notes are all the greater warrant, therefore, for ranking Edwards among the great, original minds.

But for the understanding of his intellectual history, it is not mainly important to discover the sources of his ideas. It is important rather to note that he began his life of constructive thought in philosophy, and in a philosophy grounded in reason, giving little promise of the theologian that was to be, but abundant promise of the philosopher whose mysticism should increasingly shine forth in his latest works, in part a reminiscence, in part a recovery of the impulse of his youth.

This philosophy, however, was never to yield its proper fruitage. It was arrested by emotional experiences for which Edwards himself could not account. He became a theologian of his peculiar type, not through the logical processes of his thinking, but through a kind of mystical intuition. He gives us this account of it : " I remember the time very well when I seemed to be convinced and fully satisfied as to this sovereignty of God, and his justice in thus eternally disposing of men according to his sovereign pleasure ; but never could give an account how or by what means I was thus convinced, not in the least imagining at the time, nor a long time after, that there was any extraordinary influence of God's Spirit in it, but only that now I saw further, and my mind apprehended the justness and reasonableness of it. * * * * God's absolute sovereignty and justice with respect to salvation is what my mind seems to rest assured of, as much as of anything that I see with my eyes."

Supervening upon his natural philosophical bent, such experiences, revealing a nature swayed as much by unanalyzed emotions as by reason, account for those aspects of Edwards's thought which have been noted. So potent were those experiences in their effect, that his original position was never recovered in its simplicity and originality. So disrupting were they intellectually, that his philosophy and theology remained to the close of his life almost completely divorced and unrelated. Such experiences were so consonant with Edwards's native mysticism, that one can readily understand why they never fully rose to the dignity of a contradiction in his thinking. So significant were they for his influence that we remember him, not as the greatest of American philosophers, but as the greatest of American Calvinists.

Address

THE THEOLOGY OF EDWARDS

EGBERT COFFIN SMYTH, D.D., LL.D.

Professor of Ecclesiastical History

Andover Theological Seminary

THE THEOLOGY OF EDWARDS

Edwards is too large for ordinary measuring rods. The best appreciations suggest more than is said,— are best for this reason. There is always in him something that seems to require the supposition of a fourth dimension.

You will not expect me, within the time prescribed, to review his theological treatises, nor to state in detail his doctrinal opinions, either with or without an attempt to estimate their value. I shall take the subject assigned, "The Theology of Edwards," in its strictest sense, and speak — mainly on a single line — of his Doctrine of God. But in doing this I shall endeavor to keep in mind two things,— the immediate purpose of this celebration, and what is due to Edwards in specializing in respect to any part of his thinking.

We meet to offer a sincere, grateful, intelligent tribute to his memory, to uncover anew, if we may, the sources of his power, to feel afresh the tonic influence of his vigorous and rigorous reasoning, to catch some fresh inspiration for our own busy thoughts and lives, to come again under the influence of one who was called of God to bring many of His wandering and lost children into their Father's house, and guide them to the fountains of eternal truth.

We honor him most, as we understand him best; and we best understand him as we discover how marvellously in him, mind and heart, doctrine and life, the boldest and loftiest speculation and the purest and deepest feeling were attuned, one to the other, in full rich harmony; how, in the range and variety of his inquiries and studies, and the growth and progress of his knowledge and opinions through years of intensest application and varied ministrations, there was one central thought, one controlling purpose; how, also, remarkable as is his analytic power, he seeks for wholes, and thinks and acts in wholes, as when, in his younger years, his whole soul, in a way he did not then understand, came into entire accord with the absolute sovereignty of God, or, when, the year before he died, he gave to the Trustees of the College at Princeton, as a reason for hesitancy about accepting their offer of its Presidency, that he 'had had on his mind and heart a great work, long ago begun, a History of Redemption, a body of divinity, in an entire new method, ... a method which appeared to him the most beautiful and entertaining, wherein every divine doctrine will appear to the greatest advantage, in the brightest light, in the most striking manner, showing the admirable contexture and harmony of the whole.'

"The admirable contexture and harmony of the whole," this is the key that unlocks for us the innermost chamber, discloses the central principle, of Edwards's thought.

It has been easy, in some respects to miss this. He left no *Summa Theologica*, no Body of Divinity.

His works are special Dissertations and Observations, Controversial Treatises, Sermons, a Life of Brainerd, Studies and Practical Guides in Experimental Religion. His Diary ends early. His Note Books have been seen by but few, and have not been used so as to derive from them all that is possible for a knowledge of the history of his thinking, and especially for the light they may shed upon its unity. Yet without this appreciation misunderstanding is quite sure to arise. I could say more on this point were this the appropriate occasion. If ever there was a theologian who saw a whole, and was guided and controlled by the sense of this relationship of every part or aspect of universal being and life — "the admirable contexture and harmony of the whole,"— it was Jonathan Edwards. He shed no tears, so far as we are told, when he was dismissed at Northampton, deep as was the wound inflicted, but when the council at Stockbridge decided in favor of his undertaking a most honorable work in a position of eminence and wide influence, though he had long been wonted to self-control, the tears fell.

A study of Edwards's theology which brings us into touch with its inward principle and development will naturally start with his college essay entitled "Of Being," first published by Dr. Dwight in an appendix to the Life [1]. It was characteristic of its author to seize upon this topic, and treat it as of

[1] An exact reprint may be found in the *Proceedings of the American Antiquarian Society*, Oct. 1895, pp. 241-245. See also *Ibid.*, Oct. 1896, pp. 251-252.

primary importance. Something is. "That there should absolutely be nothing at all is utterly impossible. The mind can never, let it stretch its conceptions ever so much, bring itself to conceive of a state of Perfect nothing. It puts the mind into mere Convulsion and Confusion to endeavor to think of such a state. . . . . A state of Absolute nothing is a state of Absolute Contradiction. Absolute nothing is the Aggregate of all the Absurd (?) contradictions in the World: a state wherein there is neither body, nor spirit, nor space; neither empty space nor full space; neither little nor Great, narrow nor broad; neither infinitely Great space, nor finite space, nor a mathematical point; neither Up nor Down; . . no such thing as either here or there, this way or that way, or only one way. When we go about to form an idea of Perfect nothing we must . . shut out of our minds both space that has something in it, and space that has nothing in it, . . nor must we suffer our thoughts to take sanctuary in a mathematical point. When we Go to Expel body out of Our thoughts we must Cease not to leave empty space in the Room of it, and when we go to expel emptiness from Our thoughts we must not think to squeeze it out by anything Close, hard and solid, but we must think of the same that the sleeping Rocks dream of, and not till then shall we Get a complete idea of nothing."

Something is,— Being, infinite, omnipresent, eternal, the consciousness which includes all other consciousnesses, and in which the universe has its being.

Edwards never lost this vivid sense of God, His Reality, His Immediacy. It is the first, the fundamental thing to be taken into account in an understanding of his Theology. It is requisite to a just interpretation and valuation of his controversial treatises — necessary as a knowledge of climate, of sky, soil, water-courses, to a science of the growth of flowers or forests, necessary as atmosphere to vitality. It is more instructive, for instance, to learn *how* and *why* he was so persistent and uncompromising a Determinist, could not be satisfied with what has been called " soft Determinism," than to follow his tireless logic as he chases an ambiguity or a fallacy out of the world and beyond the bounds inhabitable by any intelligence. And it is this constant sense of God, irrepressible, pouring forth in vivid metaphor and poetic image, and fervent appeal, in words of force and fire, and again of calm and sweet delight, that draws us to him, and while we are with him at once thrills and rests our spirits, as when, on a high mountain pass, or in some deep ravine, with craggy steeps and signs of Titanic elemental powers all about us, the eye rests on some perfect flower. At the heart of Edwards's most rugged and vigorous Determinism is the immediateness, the very peace, of God.

This Divine, Infinite Reality, expressed in Being, necessary to thought, implicit in all finite consciousness, is in immediate relation to the human spirit. This immediateness does not exclude mediateness,— a method of Divine revelation by symbols and types, by the ministries of Nature, prophets and priests, gospels and sacraments, by the Incarnate Word. But it does mean that all such media are of value in so far as, and only so far as, there is in them and by them in contact with our spirits the living God. Is there any other theologian in whose experience and teaching this realization of the Divine Presence is so palpable? It is the more noteworthy because never was there a divine who gave himself more diligently to the study of the written word, following it not only in perusal, but in annotation, citation, application, with persevering and tireless fidelity, nor one who surpassed him in power of analysis and deduction. Yet behind the letter and the logic, broader than the range of dialectic, and reaching farther than the subtlest discrimination of thought, is evident, as the space that holds the countless stars, the Presence to his inmost consciousness of the God he loved with a pure surpassing love and served with a marvelous consecration.

In this apprehension of the Divine as real Being, everywhere present, is implied its knowableness. One would like to see in our time a mind like that of Edwards,— or Edwards himself, if that might be,— dealing with the Agnosticism which oppresses many. How he would toss on the horns of his dialectic a scientific knowing that we do not and cannot know, that religious verities cannot be verified! Agnosticism as a belief, a knowledge, or a bar to knowledge, would seem to him like that belief in nothing which elicited his youthful polemic, and this characteristic comment: "If any man thinks that he Can think well Enough how there should be nothing I'll engage that what he means by nothing is as much something as anything that ever he thought of in his Life, and I believe that if he knew what nothing was it would be intuitively evident to him that it Could not be."

We may presume, also, that with the early Christian Apologists he would emphasize that the soul is naturally capacitated to know God, and that such knowledge has always been in some degree in its possession; that not only is it found where the Christian revelation has shed its light, but is contained in other religions as well. Such *is* his contention in one of his unpublished papers, and eagerly would he appropriate whatever progress has been made in these later days in the science of comparative religion. The testimony of prophets of Jehovah, of Christian experience, above all of Him who spake as never man spake, would flame out with surpassing splendor, for the theme would kindle his highest powers. Especially, we may believe, would he speak with reassuring tones to any who are now more or less disquieted by what is termed, rather vaguely, and sometimes a little emptily, the changed view of Scripture,— meaning, however, more particularly, new suppositions or conclusions as to the origin, construction, collection of its several books, in a word new light upon their literary history, and their relation to successive changes or stages in the religious progress of mankind.

On the one hand we may be sure that Edwards would be no less eager than the most enthusiastic scholar to learn all that can be discovered in this field of investigation, behind no one in courage and sincerity of utterance. Nor would his high idealism make him indifferent, in any degree, to historic facts, not even in the most narrow and insufficient meaning of this much abused phrase. His idealism was not subjectivism. He would recognize that there are facts with which the truth of divine revelation is bound up, which are its actual expression. Incommensurateness of fact and idea wonld not mean to him their disjunction.

Nor was he a mere mystic. No one in the history of our churches has had a greater influence on practical piety. He insisted on charity in speech and benevolence in deed. Virtue is Love. In the religious movements of which he was a leader he exhibited sanity and sagacity. It is enough to refer to his discriminating treatment of the inward testimony of the Holy Spirit. And though he did not mingle directly in political affairs, he has been credited by a recent historian with having, "more than any other man, settled the principle which fully justified to the American mind the complete severance of the State from ecclesiastical functions or concern." [1]

Yet, on the other hand, it is noteworthy, as the author to whom I have just referred points out, that this service was rendered, not directly, but through Edwards's religious teaching.[2] And it would still doubtless be on this line, and with this power, that he would influence, if living among us, the doubt and distrust of our time. "The gospel," he wrote, after witnessing, analysing, and studying in many forms its divine power,—"The gospel of the blessed God does not go abroad a begging for its evidence so much as some think: it has its highest and most proper evidence in itself."[3] "Unless men may come to a reasonable solid persuasion and conviction of the truth of the gospel . . . . by a sight of its glory, it is impossible that those who are illiterate, and unacquainted with history should have any thorough and effectual conviction of it at all. . . . . After all that learned men have said to them, there will remain innumerable doubts on their minds; they will be ready, when pinched with some great trial of their faith, to say 'How do I know this or that? How do I know when these histories were written? Learned men . . . . tell me there is equal reason to believe these facts, as any whatsoever that are related at such a distance; but how

---

[1] *The Rise of Religious Liberty in America, A History.* By Sanford H. Cobb, N. Y. The Macmillan Co., 1902. Page 485.

[2] *Ib.*, pp. 485-486.

[3] *Treatise on Religious Affections*, Sect. V., I. *Works*, Vol. V., p. 186; ed. Dwight.

do I know that other facts which are related of those ages ever were?'"[1]

Edwards's solution of the difficulty of the unlearned is good for all. The scholar needs it as well as others. Still the gospel is its own best evidence; its demonstration is "the demonstration of the Spirit and of power." Edwards knew this gospel by its supreme result in character and life; knew it in his own protracted, analysed, tested, profound experience; saw it in a life, united with his own, so constant in cheerfulness, benevolence, devoutness, divine communion, that its spiritual raptures seem scarcely more wonderful than it would have been had they not been vouchsafed; observed it in its effect in many places and successive seasons, in persons of various ranks, callings and ages, and this with as keen a psychological eye as one may read of, quickened in its watchfulness by a profound sense of responsibility; and in these impressive and memorable words he gives us his testimony both as to the reality and value of the knowledge the gospel imparts: "He that sees the beauty of holiness, or true moral good, sees the greatest and most important thing in the world. . . . Unless this is seen nothing is seen that is worth the seeing; for there is no other true excellency or beauty. Unless this be understood, nothing is understood worthy the exercise of the noble faculty of understanding. This is the beauty of the Godhead, the divinity of divinity

[1] *Ibid.*, pp. 182-183.

(if I may so speak), the good of the infinite fountain of good. Without this, God Himself (if that were possible) would be an infinite evil; we ourselves had better never have been, and there had better have been no being. He therefore in effect knows nothing that knows not this; his knowledge is but the shadow of knowledge, or the *form of knowledge*, as the apostle calls it. . . . . And well may regeneration, in which this divine sense is given to the soul by its Creator, be represented as opening the blind eyes, raising the dead, and bringing a person into a new world."[1]

Edwards included in what may be known of God His existence as Father, Son, and Holy Spirit. In the editions of his collected works there is no formal discussion of this subject. The doctrine, however, plainly appears in various aspects, particularly in affecting representations of the excellence and glory of the Redeemer, and discriminating discussions of the work of the Holy Spirit. In general it may be said that it pervades his system of theology, so that this would be unintelligible without it. The doctrine, in a word, is present in his published writings, as it generally is in Holy Scripture, that is, in obvious presuppositions, implications, and practical applications. It sheds light upon the most intimate and profound experiences revealed in the Christian consciousness, and is implied in manifold known operations and effects pertaining to the life of the

[1] *Ibid.*, p. 158.

children of God. It makes the *via crucis* a *via lucis*. It belongs to the far, high, pure, ever burning lights that guide upward to the immediate vision of Him all whose blessedness and majesty and glory, with the entire good of the universe, are involved and insured in this, that He is eternally and essentially Father, Son, and Holy Ghost.

In the delightful "Treatise on Grace," printed for private circulation by Mr. Grosart, Edwards says, "Though the word person be rarely used in the Scriptures, yet I believe that we have no word in the English language that does so naturally represent what the Scripture reveals of the distinction of the eternal Three,— Father, Son, and Holy Ghost — as to say, they are one God, but three persons."[1] He recognizes also the mystery of the doctrine, and our dependence for knowledge and guidance respecting it on Sacred Scripture, which, he says,— referring directly to an inquiry into the nature of the Holy Spirit,—"certainly should be our rule in matters so much above reason and our own notions."[2]

In Manuscripts mostly as yet unpublished, either in whole or in part, are numerous papers on the subject. I may say in passing that when in this address I use the term "Observation," or "Observations," for a source of information respecting Edwards's opinions, I refer to statements derived from these Manuscripts.

[1] *Op. cit.*, p. 43.
[2] *Ib.*, pp. 43, 47.

THE THEOLOGY OF EDWARDS

How often we come closest to some great leader, in his deepest thoughts and aims, as a biographer gives us a glimpse of his youth, its intuitions, perceptions, aspirations, dreams. The key to the life usually hangs in that closet. Whatever critics may conclude, the Church will always be profoundly grateful for the picture in the Third Gospel of the Child Jesus among the doctors.

A study of the *Observations* of Edwards shows that deep thoughts upon the Trinity came to him in the beginnings of his theological studies, indeed, some paragraphs in the published Series entitled "The Mind," in all probability carry us back yet farther.[1] It appears, also, that for a number of years, perhaps down close upon the time when he must have been much absorbed in labors connected with the "Revival," and the "Great Awakening," and again after he had left Northampton, that is to the last, the same theme engaged his thought.[1] Nowhere is there any indication of dissatisfaction with the accepted historic doctrine. Rather it is an endeavor, by what the writer himself regards as intense thought, to bring the doctrine more clearly to

---

[1] See No. 1. EXCELLENCY [Dwight's, ed. I. pp. 696, 697]; also, No. 45, Paragraphs 1, 2, 4, 9, 12 [*Ib.*, pp. 699, 700, 701]. The earliest Observation on the Trinity in the series entitled "Miscellanies" is numbered 94, which is equivalent to 142. The number 52 is usually added to those in this series on account of its beginning with the alphabet,—first a single letter, then double letters. But I find that there is no *j* nor *jj*, also no *v* nor *vv*, so that the added number should be 48. No. 1, of Series "The Mind," is apparently, unless "Of Being" is prior, the earliest college composition by Edwards of which we have any knowledge. It was probably composed in his Sophomore or early in his Junior year. It contains the germ of his many subsequent philosophical remarks upon the Trinity. No. 94 (142) of the "Miscellanies" is supposed to have been written towards the close of his residence at the College as a graduate student (1720-1722), and before his Tutorship. See Dwight, I. p. 56; also *Appendix I.* to this volume, No. A.

view, and this by seeing it as reflected in the mirror of self-consciousness. The attempt was not novel, but it is remarkable in its clearness of conception, and in its presentation and answering of objections.

I had prepared a statement of its positions and method, with quotations from hitherto unused documents, but must omit the reading, that I may allude to other topics.[1] What is most striking, for myself I should say instructive and helpful, in the discussions is the clear conviction, the fearless claim of the Reasonableness of the doctrine from the point of view of what the writer calls "naked Reason," the repeated assertion of the power of human reason to deal with the subject, and the foundation of the claim in a broader view of the likeness of man to God. In the human spirit there is a three-fold distinction which is a resemblance to the Trinity of the Divine Nature. I may not conceal my impression that it would have been happy for the New England Theology, at least, and the interests it represents, if Edwards's thoughts on this subject had obtained an earlier and wider publicity. I must, however, add with equal frankness and distinctness that I have no suspicion that they have ever been withheld from any doubt as to the writer's Trinitarianism.

For the reason already suggested I must omit what I had written respecting his treatment of the Incarnation,— except to say that the same principle which guides his thought on the Trinity is applied

[1] See *Appendix I*. A.

by him to this doctrine. I refer to the principle of man's likeness to his Maker. Edwards thus recognizes distinctly and interestedly, what has become a first principle in our later and best Christologies.[1] He does not, however, follow out this principle to its legitimate results in our conception of the Divine method of recovering men to God. That which is essential in the constitution of the Redeemer's Person must be fundamental in our interpretation of what He is and does for us as our Redeemer. There is, through the Divine Creative Son, who became man, a natural sonship of man to God which must have a place in our thought of the sonship which is by grace. To have missed this application of his own principle may be regarded as a chief immediate cause both of what was most excessive and defective in Edwards's teaching.

His thought of God is still further disclosed to us in his interpretation of the revealed Purpose or End of God in Creation. His "Dissertation" on this topic, which ranks with his principal works, was written, it is supposed, for publication, though it did not appear until several years after his decease. From notes found among his papers it was conjectured that he was thinking of some revision of it, but no evidence has appeared that he was meditating any material change.

The *Observations* contain numerous papers on the same theme, running from his early days into the

[1] See *Appendix I*. B.

years at Stockbridge. In these manuscripts we overhear Edwards saying to himself in his study substantially what is expressed in the "Dissertation." The light of the one blends harmoniously with that of the other. Yet there is in the unpublished series a fascinating variety and freshness of utterance, and as we follow in them the growth of his thought, we come in some respects into closer intimacy with it, and are impressed with its richness and fulness.

Several questions have arisen in the interpretation of the "Dissertation."

Does its author regard happiness as the End? Does he subordinate virtue to happiness? Does he understand, in making the glory of God the End, that receiving glory is what is aimed at, so that the "apparent effect" of what is said is, the glorification of "an infinite and celestial selfishness?" Was he perplexed in thought, when he wrote the "Dissertation," by seeing before him, in his recoil from Deism, a menacing pantheism? And for relief was he in his last years, turning for the first time to the "Christian doctrine of the Trinity?"

I think, after examining the *Observations* as well as reading anew the "Dissertation," that these questions must all be answered in the negative, although Happiness no doubt enters largely into Edwards's thought of the Divine Purpose.

The *Observations* are most emphatic in their evidence that Edwards's thought is not that God's chief end in creation is that of receiving glory. His conception is precisely the opposite. His fundamental thought of God,— one that he connects again and again with Creation,— is that of a Being whose absolute Perfection implies self-impartation, reciprocity, mutual Love, which itself is an energy so intense and complete that into it as an act of intercommunication is poured the fullness of Infinite Being. This conception of the Trinity Edwards early and late connects with the Creation of the Universe. God does not create to meet a deficiency in his own nature, but just the contrary. He creates because of the plenitude of His Being, as a full fountain overflows. His glory is to give. He creates to communicate,— to give *Himself*, to be the creature's good.[1]

Edwards taught nothing new in presenting the glory of God as the End of the Creation, but he greatly enriched its interpretation. He smote the rock, and the living waters flowed. With the blessing of God he made the truth productive of noblest service, in our churches at home and on many a mission field, from men who lived to glorify God. And into what simplicity, purity, disinterestedness of motive, and inward tranquility, and liberation of energies of consecrated service, they came in the divine communion into which their spirits were brought. Life under the sternest skies, on the stormiest seas, in the farthest wildernesses, was under

[1] See *Appendix I. C.*

the care and guidance of a Power known in their own reason and deepest experience to be supreme. The Universe was their Friend, sustaining them, moving them ever onward, as, by a returning voyager, his ship beneath his feet is felt, with a thrill of joy, to be bearing him, with the whole momentum of its mighty mass, HOMEWARD.

Homeward to God, whose we are and from whom we came — this is the innermost meaning and the climax of Edwards's Theology.

We may get a better doctrine of the Will than he maintained, though never without him, for he has made forever secure in thought the doctrine of motive. We may widen our conceptions beyond his ken in respect to the methods of divine grace, — its approaches, and the opportunities of receiving it, but well will it be with us if we come as fully as he under the constraining power of such love, and drink as deeply at its celestial springs.

I had intended to say something on Edwards's views of Divine Sovereignty, on his Determinism, perhaps on his severities, — but it is impossible. The problem of Liberty and Necessity, like that of Realism and Idealism, is not merely one of Psychology. It must be solved, if at all, in the realm of Philosophy. Edwards rises to this higher level. It is his native air. His conception of Perfect Being contains the Trinity, his thought of personal freedom merges in the Liberty of the sons of God. We have broken with him, and shall do so again and again, but anon shall look and see him on some higher range, above our clouds. The deepest philosophical and religious thought of our time, on most important lines, if I mistake not, is moving upward on the way which led him in thought to God.

Homeward to God — this is indeed the sum of Edwards's Theology; yet I should be unjust to one who saw all divinity comprised in a History of Redemption, if I did not add, Homeward by Him who came to seek and to save the lost, Christ and Him crucified. Edwards summons us to know God by Reason, — yet by Faith. Would he not say: See Him, know Him, and yourself, and all besides, through the eyes that opened in the manger, turned with compassion to the multitude, looked on Peter in his sin, and closed on the cross to open again upon a world redeemed.

Poem

A WITNESS TO THE TRUTH

BY

SAMUEL VALENTINE COLE, D.D.

President of Wheaton Seminary

A WITNESS TO THE TRUTH

I.

God's truth has many voices; sun and star
And mountain and the deep that rolls afar,
Speak the great language; and, of mightier worth,
The lips and lives of Godlike men on earth.

For truth wrought out in human life has power
Which no truth else has — since man's natal hour.
What were the world without the long, strong chain
Of faithful witnesses, whose heart and brain
Have throbbed with truth God gave them? without these
Who, as with hands that link together, stand
Reaching across the years to that dear Hand
Which touched blind eyes to sight, wrote on the sand,
And lifted Peter from the drowning seas?
Who, better than through book or hymn or creed,
Draw down their living line the fire we need
Of life from Him who is the Life indeed?

II.

A good man's work is of his time and place
Where Duty lifts the fulness of her face;
Translate it elsewhere and you do him wrong;
His life, his spirit — what of great and fair
And true was in him — O, that doth belong
To all the ages and dwells everywhere!

And there he stands, this nobly-moulded man;
You can not miss him if you turn and scan
The land's horizon; howsoe'er men talk,
He still is of us; no mere name; a rock
The floods may beat upon nor wash away;
Foregatherer of the times; his loftier height
Flushed with the gleams of sweetness and of light
That wait their fulness till some later day;
An eagle spirit soaring in the sky
And mingling with the things that can not die.

How full of fire he was, and how sincere,
Soldier of faith and conscience without fear!
And humble as the little springtime flower
Opening its heart out to the Heavenly Power;
Poet, and dreamer of the things to be;
A man of Godly vision; — such was he,
This Dante of New England, who descried
The dread Inferno of man's sin and pride;
The Purgatorio where his eyes might trace
The workings out and upward of God's grace;
And yet who clomb with happier step the slope
Of man's aspiring and undying hope
Toward Paradiso, there to find his goal
At last, — the Blessed Vision of the Soul!

III.

All this he was, whatever be the name
He goes by in the roll of earthly fame.

A WITNESS TO THE TRUTH

We judge him as we would ourselves alway
Be judged; as Christ will judge the world one day;
Not by things done, however great they be,
But by those longings which immortally
Outrun achievement since the world began;
Yea, by the spirit in him; that's the man.

What though the vain world scoffed and paths grew dim,
He had one Master and he followed Him.
He wielded truth to meet the age's stress
Of circumstance, nor made it truth the less.
Truth is a sword that flashes, now this way,
Now that, the single purpose to obey.
Nay, truth is large; no man hath seen the whole;
Larger than words; it brooks not the control
Of argument and of distinctions nice;
No age or creed can hold it, no device
Of speech or language; ay, no syllogism:
Truth is the sun, and reasoning is the prism
You lift before it; whence the light is thrown
In various colors; each man takes his own.
If this man takes the red, as you the blue,
Is yours the whole? and is his truth not true?
Spirit is truth, howe'er the colors fall;
The fact comes back to spirit after all.

IV.

Secure, invincible, the man who dare
Obey his vision — mark what courage there! —

Dare take the sword of his belief in hand,
Whole-hearted face the world with it, and stand,
And mind not sacrifice, and count fame dross,
For truth's dear sake, and life and all things loss,
And never dream of failure, never doubt
What issue when the stars of God come out!

And would that we had power like him to rise
Clear of the thraldom of all compromise,
Like him whose feet on this foundation stood, —
That God is sovereign and that God is good.
Is such a creed outworn? And tell me, pray,
Have we no use for it? Alas the day,
Amid the things that savor of the sod,
If men forget the sovereign rights of God!
The true life's master-word is still, Obey.

V.

The man of power rejoicing cries, "I can;"
  "I may," the man of pleasure; but we trust,
And all the world trusts with us, still the man
  Hearing a different voice, who says, "I must."

O Conscience, Conscience, how we need thee now!
  Wind, fire, and earthquake pass; the time abounds
In these great voices; but, O, where art thou?
  Is thy voice lost amid life's grosser sounds?

Or art thou fled across the golden bars
  Of evening with thy purer light to shine
Somewhere far off, beyond the quiet stars,
  Far off, and leave us without guide or sign?

Not so; earth's towers and battlements decay;
  Thrones tremble and fall; old sceptres lose control;
But, as God lives, thou livest; thou wilt stay,
  O Conscience, God's vicegerent in the soul.

We are thy bondmen and thy ways are good;
  Thou art what makes us greater than the dust
We came from; and still, howsoe'er we would,
  Thy law is ever on us and we must.

VI.

The man who takes "an inward sweet delight
In God," shines like a candle in the night;
The world's black shadow of care and doubt and sin
Is beaten backward by that power within;
He walks in freedom; neither time nor place
Can fetter such a spirit; in his face
A light, not of this earth, forever clings;
For, when he will, strong spiritual wings
Bear him aloft, till silent grows all strife,
Silent the tumult and the toil of life;
The homes of men, far off, like grains of sand
Lie scattered along the wrinkles of the land,
All silent; not a sound or breath may rise

To mar the eternal harmony of those skies
Through which he goes, still higher, toward the line
Where sun and moon have no more need to shine;
And there, where sordid feet have never trod,
He walks in joy the table-lands of God.

VII.

How much he hath to teach us even yet,
Lest life should kill us with its toil and fret!
Things of the earth men seek to have and hold;
They build and waste again their mounds of gold.
O me! the din of life, the bell that peals,
The traffic, and the roaring of the wheels!
Work glows and grows and satisfies us not;
Weary we are of what our hands have wrought,
Weary of action with no time for thought.
The much we do — how little it must count
Without some pattern showed us in the mount!

Who seeks and loves the company of great
Ideals, and moves among them, soon or late
Will learn their ways and language, unaware
Take on their likeness, ay, and some day share
Their immortality, as this man now
Before whose life we reverently bow.

VIII.

So shines the lamp of Edwards; still it sends
One golden beam down the long track of years,

A WITNESS TO THE TRUTH

This resolute truth which neither yields nor spends, —
That life, true life, is not of what appears,
Not of the things the world piles wide and high;
'Tis of the spirit and will never die.

His life was noble; wherefore let the day
White with his memory shine beside the way —
Adding its comfort to our human need —
Like some fair tablet whereon men may read:
" Lo, here and there, great witnesses appear, —
The meek, the wise, the fearless, the sincere;
They live their lives and witness to the word;
No time so evil but their voice is heard;
Nor sword nor flame can stop them; though they die
They grow not silent; they must cry their cry;
Time's many a wave breaks dying on the shore;
They cry forever and forevermore;
For, in and through such men as these men are,
God lives and works, and it were easier far
To dry the seas and roll the mountains flat,
Than banish God; we build our hopes on that."

Address

THE INFLUENCE OF EDWARDS

JAMES ORR, D.D.

Professor of Theology, United Free Church College

Glasgow

THE INFLUENCE OF EDWARDS

To speak of Jonathan Edwards to a company of New Englanders, still more to speak of him within the walls of an institution built in a manner to enshrine his memory and perpetuate his influence, is an adventurous task for one whose home is in another continent, and whose religious associations are different from those by which you are encircled. Yet there may be a fitness in one from another land being present at this interesting celebration, to bear to you greeting, and to testify that we in Scotland are not unmindful of the mighty debt we owe to New England — which in truth all Christendom owes — for the gift of a consecrated genius of such rare power and enduring influence as his whom you today commemorate. The name of Jonathan Edwards is one which entwines itself with the oldest recollections of many of us. We met with it in biography, in the literature of religion, in text-books and prelections in philosophy, in divinity systems, in allusions to the influence of Edwards on the thought and lives of other men; and, though one's ideas were sometimes vague enough of the man himself and of his actual surroundings and struggles at a time when, politically and religiously, everything in New England was yet in the making, the impression made upon us was always one of veneration for his character, admiration for his extraordinary genius, and awe at the searching spiritual power of his words.

If I may indulge in reminiscence, it is forty years and more since I first made my own serious acquaintance with Edwards in poring over his treatise on *The Freedom of the Will* (I think it was as holiday reading: I have a dim memory connecting it with a gooseberry garden in Kilmarnock!), and I have no doubt that the trains of thought then set in motion have continued to vibrate in my conscious or subliminal self till the present hour. It is to myself a singular satisfaction to be on the very soil from which he sprang, amidst the scenes and the people among whom, generations ago, he lived his laborious and devoted life, and to stand tonight in this honourable gathering, surrounded by mementos of his influence, where the one object is to do him honour.

How could one contract any other sentiment than that of reverence for Jonathan Edwards, when his name was never mentioned by any distinguished writer except with highest eulogy of his intellectual and moral eminence? That theologians like Andrew Fuller, Robert Hall, and Thomas Chalmers — all of whom acknowledge their indebtedness to him, and in all of whom his influence is distinctly to be traced — should place him on this high pedestal is perhaps not to be wondered at; but when writers in pure philosophy, in no way enamoured of his special doctrines, — as, *e. g.*, Sir James Mackintosh,

Dugald Stewart, F. D. Maurice, and even the German Fichte, — speak of his metaphysical genius in praise and astonishment, it is difficult to resist the conviction that here is a phenomenon in the history of mind worth turning aside to see. You, in your own New England theology, prolonged through so many phases, yet dominated throughout by the influence of Edwards, furnish a measure of the range and profundity of that influence which suffices of itself to show how many-sided, forceful, and germinal it has been. And in this connection, as I have named F. D. Maurice, I may be permitted, before going further, to quote a sentence or two of his, which, coming from so impartial a mind, may be felt to be apposite to the present occasion :

"In his own country," Mr. Maurice says, "he (Edwards) retains, and must always retain a great power. We should imagine that all American theology and philosophy, whatever changes it may undergo, and with whatever foreign elements it may be associated, must be cast in his mould. New Englanders who try to substitute Berkeley, or Butler, or Malebranche, or Condillac, or Kant, or Hegel, for Edwards, and to form their minds upon any of them, must be forcing themselves into an unnatural position, and must suffer in the effort. On the contrary, if they accept the starting-point of their native teacher, and seriously consider what is necessary to make that teacher consistent with himself — what is necessary that the divine foundation upon which he wished to build may not be too weak and narrow for any human or social life to rest upon it — we should expect great and fruitful results from these inquiries to the land which they care for most, and therefore to mankind." (*Moral and Metaphysical Philosophy*, II. 472.)

I shall now, with your permission, come to closer quarters, and shall try to state briefly for myself the impression I have been led to form of this great thinker's genius and influence. It is customary to place the supremacy of Edwards in his unrivalled metaphysical acuteness; and even so appreciative a critic as Henry Rogers resolves his greatness almost exclusively into the possession, in unsurpassed degree, of the ratiocinative faculty—of Reason. "*In this respect*, at least," he says, "he well deserves the emphatic admiration which Robert Hall expressed when he somewhat extravagantly said that Edwards was 'the greatest of the sons of men.'" But this is at least one-sided. I shall not dwell, as I should wish to do, on the singularly powerful influence which Edwards has exercised, in his personality and published writings, through the simple force of his pure and intense *godliness*, but shall content myself with saying that it will be difficult, in the long list of saints and mystics, to point to one in whom the pure light of intellect was more intimately united with the pure glow of love to God in the heart — with habitual, sustained, all-pervading, spiritual affection. One has only to study the fragmentary records of his early resolutions and private experiences, and the parts of his writings which deal with experimental religion, to see how entirely in him the white light is one with white heat. I name the state of his soul *godliness*; for while his mind was filled, as few have been, with a realization of the beauty and excellence of Christ, and with the sense of obligation to Christ in redemption, it is still, ultimately, God's love from which salvation is always viewed as flowing, and *to* God, as the supreme object of affection, that everything in salvation is regarded as leading back; while love to God, contemplation of his excellence, and assimilation to his holiness, are the supreme elements in the soul's blessedness.

The intellectual and spiritual or mystical powers in Edwards, therefore, exist in inseparable union, and even his speculative insight — which is, despite Mr. Rogers, far more than mere logical or ratiocinative acuteness — cannot rightly be understood, if divorced from the spiritual perception from which a large part of its light arises. There is at the same time nothing mystical, in the *wrong* sense of the word, in Edwards's spirituality, for it is never cut away from the historical; neither is there anything about it fanatical and visionary, for it has its root in humility, is checked by the most vigorous self-analysis, and is in essence a pure aspiration after God and holiness. Listen only to this, relating to the years after his conversion:

"My longings after God and holiness were much

increased. Pure and humble, holy and heavenly, Christianity appeared exceedingly amiable to me. I felt a burning desire to be, in everything, a complete Christian; and conformed to the blessed image of Christ; and that I might live in all things, according to the pure, sweet, and blessed rules of the Gospel. I had an eager thirsting after progress in these things; which put me upon pursuing and pressing after them . . . . I remember the thoughts I used then to have of holiness; and said sometimes to myself, 'I do certainly know that I love holiness, such as the Gospel prescribes.' It appeared to me there was nothing in it but what was ravishingly lovely; the highest beauty and amiableness — a divine beauty; far purer here upon earth; and that everything else was like mire and defilement in comparison with it."

Nature itself was transfigured to this man of spiritual vision; its objects and glories became as it were a pure transparency, through which was visible only the Divine excellency. Can anyone wonder at the strange spiritual fascination of such a book as that on the Religious Affections, coming from a soul so penetrated with love to God? We think of Fenelon and Madame Guyon, but Edwards's piety burned with as pure a flame as theirs, while it was largely free from the morbid and quietistic elements which marred their sainthood.

Having, however, premised these things, I am prepared to go as far as any — perhaps farther than most — in my appreciation of the supreme metaphysical faculty of Edwards, and of the influence he has exercised on subsequent thought through that. I have already said that it is not correct to speak of Edwards's intellectual superiority as consisting merely in unrivalled ratiocinative ability. Jonathan Edwards has the intuitive gift; he is a great metaphysical, not less than a great spiritual, idealist. His nature instinctively soars; the higher the tracts in which his thought moves, the freer its action. David Hume was a precocious speculator, but the few pages of notes and discussions on Mind, penned by Edwards under the impulse of his first study of Locke, in his sixteenth or seventeenth year, seem to me as remarkable in metaphysical subtlety as anything in Hume, while, in the spirit that informs them, they are on a far higher level. The singular thing is that, in keeping with what has been said of his idealistic bent, Edwards, in these notes, and, so far as appears, independently, works out a theory of idealism closely akin to Berkeley's, sustaining it by arguments, and meeting objections with a skill that must evoke the admiration of everyone familiar with the subject. When one reflects that the Berkelean idealism is pretty much the *pons asinorum* of the student of philosophy, getting safely over which, he may justly be credited with some degree of philosophical νοῦς, it will be felt that for a youth like Edwards, thrown almost entirely upon his own resources, to work out this theory as he has done, or, even if chance had thrown some work of Berkeley's in his way, (which does not seem to have been the case), to appropriate and reproduce its thoughts so admirably, was a noteworthy achievement.

It is not, however, only in his theory of the external world, and of God as the cause of our perceptions, that Edwards displays his metaphysical faculty; his remarks on space, time, substance, cause, are equally acute and mature. There is, it is not too much to say, as much pure metaphysical thinking packed up in this score or so of pages, as would set up many a modern thinker for life; and had Edwards chosen to follow out this line, and had he, like Hume, reduced his speculations to the form of a book, his place in philosophy would perhaps have been as high as his.

Edwards, however, did better than I have suggested both for himself and for us; for philosophy to him was at no time an end in itself, but was valued only as it led back to, or had relations with, God and religion. The converse of this is also true, that religion, as it moves back on ultimate questions, always becomes to him again a kind of philosophy; is lifted up into a region of more or less lofty speculation. Here, in discussing such subjects, *e. g.*, as the last end of God in creation, the relation of eternity to time, the ground of virtue in disinterested love of being, the freedom of the will, Edwards is at his loftiest and best; the language of the schools is dropped, and we move in a region of pure abstract thought. To follow him in the highest of these flights needs the eye of the eagle that is not afraid to gaze on the sun.

The work by which Edwards is best known as a metaphysician throughout all lands is probably his treatise on *The Freedom of the Will*. In the mere *matter* of this famous treatise, over which so much ink has been spilt, I do not suppose that there is much that is absolutely new. It could easily be shown, I think, that its leading ideas, and practically all its arguments in favour of philosophical necessity, had been anticipated by previous writers. What gives Edwards's book its classic distinction is not its novelty, but the cool, dialetical precision with which the argument, as a whole, is presented; the skill with which point after point is driven home; the close concatenation of all its parts; the phalanxed order with which, from opening to close, his reasoning marches to its inevitable conclusion. I do not say that Edwards succeeds in satisfying us, or that no flaws can be pointed out in his argument, firmly riveted as it is. Will is not simply prevailing desire; nor is self-determination to be got rid of by conjuring up the supposed necessity of an infinite series of self-determining acts. I suppose everyone feels, when the utmost has been said in favour of the necessity of volition, that there is still an *irreducible element* in consciousness — a something that escapes logic — in which yet the essence of our personality and moral freedom lies. Still, if the question is taken on the ground of strict logic — if it is asked, for instance, Is Will absolutely lawless in its action? Is there any volition for which, if we get to the bottom of the act, there is not a *why*? Or, if such a thing could be, would it not be something irrational, an act utterly unaccountable, that could, as Edwards says, neither be foreknown by God nor relied on by man? — if questions like these are put, it is difficult indeed to refute Edwards, or the subtler forms of psychological and metaphysical determinism that have appeared since his time. It is at any rate a curious fact that it is the greater metaphysical minds that seem almost always driven to determinism — Locke, Spinoza, Leibnitz; Hobbes and Hume, of course; Kant on the theoretic side; Hegel, from the absolute point of view; Spencer, and with him the greater number of our scientific thinkers. I must not dare to discuss the problem here; only Edwards will still be of use to us if he warns us from the danger of superficial conclusions.

One thing, however, in Edwards's presentation, which I regard as seriously defective, I should like to lay my finger on. It is not his own; it is borrowed from Locke; it is in plainest conflict with his own deepest philosophy. All the more need is there on that account that it should be pointed out. It is the proposition, assumed as an axiom, that "the will always is as the greatest apparent good is," that the good is "of the same import with [the] agreeable," — that "to appear good to the mind is the same as to appear agreeable;" — that evil, on the contrary, is "that which is disagreeable and uneasy." "Agreeable" or "pleasing," here, of course, is agreeable or pleasing to the subject concerned — to the agent willing. Strictly construed, this would reduce ethics to eudaemonism, and that of a type in which the happiness which determines action is always one's own happiness, not another's. I need hardly say that nothing could be further from Edwards's own doctrine of the foundation of virtue in disinterested benevolence, or from what he elsewhere says of the possession by the agent of "a moral faculty, or sense of good and evil [not here, observe, meaning agreeable or its reverse] . . . . and a capacity which an agent has of being influenced in his actions by moral inducements or motives, exhibited to the view of understanding and reason, to engage to a conduct agreeable to the moral faculty." Not that I can accept, without qualification, Edwards's doctrine of the nature of virtue — noble as it is — but the necessary qualifications he himself, I think it could be shown, abundantly supplies in his doctrine of rectitude, and the obligations arising out of fitness in the relations of moral beings.

I hasten from philosophy to theology, and here so vast a field opens itself to view, that I despair of doing more than simply casting a glance at a few of the greater streams of influence that have issued from this abounding source. One thing that at once strikes the reader of Edwards in this connection is the immense distance the mind has travelled within the last two hundred years — or let us say within the last forty or fifty years — from the theological standpoint which his works represent. How are we, it may be asked, to enter with any intelligence or sympathy into questions about original sin and Adam's relation to his posterity — we, who are today discussing whether there ever was an Adam, or have exchanged the Adam for our scientific ancestor, Mr. Darwin's "hairy-tailed quadruped, probably arboreal in its habits, and an inhabitant of the ancient world,"; who, instead of original sin, speak of "our brute inheritance", which the travail of the ages has been thus far unsuccessful in throwing off? I acknowledge the contrast; I know that we have outgrown much that belongs to the fashion of a past age in thought and speech, and in our modes of using Scripture; but I do not, therefore, own that Jonathan Edwards has become obsolete, or is of no living value to us today. Just because the thoughts with which his mind was perpetually occupied were the highest and grandest, — just because the questions to which he pierced down were the basal ones of all religion, — they must, like the perennial stars, retain their interest and fascination for us amidst all the vicissitudes in mundane opinion. There is a permanent element in them because they deal with the eternal.

It may be taken for granted that there never will

come a time when men cease to revolve the problem of God's last end in creation, or are likely to find a sublimer and more satisfying answer than that given in Edwards's famous dissertation. We have our modern re-handlings of the doctrine of sin, but the questions will recur — What *is* sin? Is the "brute inheritance" after all an adequate explanation of it? How does sin come to be here, and what is the holy God's relation to it? On these subjects Edwards will open up to us depths, which, whether we accept all his own solutions or not, we shall be forced to confess that the ordinary evolutionary text-books have no line long enough to fathom. Our author would find no relief in the idea that man came into existence in a state in which the animal propensities had almost undivided sway in his nature. You don't, he would say, show how man *became* sinful, but you start him off on this hypothesis already sinful. For a moral being in this turbulent, anarchic state — immersed in a life of unregulated passion — is already in a *wrong* moral state — wrong for *him*. The opponent might retort that if so, he was in a wrong moral state by "an arbitrary constitution of God," and Edwards might have difficulty in repelling this use of one of his own arguments against himself.

Yet how subtle are some of his ideas even in this obscure region? If we get to the inwardness of his theories, we perceive that many of them depend really on his original idealistic premises. His theory of identity, *e. g.*, as consisting in a continual new creation, — how could it be otherwise, if substance has no independent existence, and if properties subsist only through the continual exertion of the thought and will of God? The exercise-theory of Dr. Emmons finds here, in fact, a very logical justification. Or, again, that constituted identity of Adam and his descendants, in virtue of which they form one great moral person — how curiously does idealism here turn round to a species of organic realism, the type of which, in Edwards's own image, is the tree and its branches? And how curiously also does physiological science, as represented say by Weissmann, with its latest novelty of the discovery — or alleged discovery — of an undying germ-plasm in the living species, give to his theory of a single race-life a quasi-corroboration?

What impresses one on the large scale in Edwards is the exceeding grandeur, but hardly less the strange contrasts, and often scarcely veiled antinomies of his thought. On the one hand, how grand the sweep of his thought, as it swings on the pivot of the divine sovereignty, in the midst of the eternities, between the two great poles of sin and redemption! Yet, on the other, how difficult to reconcile this conception of naked sovereignty either with his own idea of freedom, or with his doctrine of the supremacy of love in God's nature and purpose! In this doctrine of what Dorner calls the "teleological" relation of love to the other divine attributes, Edwards held in his hands the means of correcting the harshness of the older Calvinism, without sacrificing anything of its truth; but he failed to use it. The same contrast meets us in other respects. How strangely penetrated the soul of Edwards was by the love of God, — how entirely love was to him the end of creation, the essence of virtue, God's very being; yet how terrible his view of the divine justice, how awful his pictures of sin and of hell! On this a word immediately.

On the doctrines of applied redemption — justification, regeneration, sanctification, — there is perhaps not much that needs to be said; but on the doctrine of atonement, or as Edwards calls it, "Christ's satisfaction for sin," it is not too much to say that, with outward and entirely sincere adherence to the old formulas, Edwards is a path-finder, and inaugurates a new period in the treatment of that doctrine. I pass over New England developments, which are much better known to you than they can be to me, and refer to the exceptional influence his germinal ideas have had through one of the most original and spiritual thinkers of the Scottish Church, Dr. John McLeod Campbell. Campbell stands in direct affiliation to Edwards. He connects himself directly with a suggestion of Edwards that there are conceivably two ways in which satisfaction for sin might have been made — "either," as he expresses it, "an equivalent punishment or an equivalent sorrow and repentance";

and himself accepts the second of these two ways as that in which the atonement *has* been made (a view which Edwards rejected). Christ, he thinks, presented to God on men's behalf "an adequate sorrow and repentance"—a quite untenable conception. In reality, however, this formula does not express the central and essential thing in Campbell's theory, and his view, when closely scrutinized, is found closely to resemble Edwards's own. The view of Edwards he expounds and defends from objections, and in its essence accepts.

Edwards's own statement, however, is, it seems to me, the more complete, scriptural, and adequate of the two. While granting that Christ passed truly under the judgment of God in enduring the death threatened against sin, he yet lays the whole stress, in explaining the atoning virtue of these sufferings, on the moral and spiritual elements contained in them, and so in effect transforms the doctrine of atonement from within. Christ is the divine and human mediator, who, standing between God and man, is able perfectly to enter into the mind of both, and to identify himself with both with perfect sympathy. On the one hand, he has a full apprehension of the sin of man, and of its evil desert; on the other, he enters fully into the mind of God regarding sin, and into the realization of the wrath which is its due. He thus truly, yet inwardly and not merely by legal imputation, bore our sins, rendering through his inward acknowledgement of the justice of God in the condemnation of sin a tribute to the divine righteousness, which makes reparation for the guilt humanity has incurred. McLeod Campbell, in his expressive way, speaks of this as the "Amen" which went up from the humanity of Jesus in response to the divine mind about sin, in which lay the essence of atonement. I myself think that in these utterances of Edwards and Campbell we possibly touch the deepest meaning of the Cross in its expiatory and propitiatory aspect.

The admiration I have expressed for the genius and character of Edwards is not to be construed as if I were insensible of the limitations that inhere in the piety and thought of this truly great and saintly man. I refer only to two points in closing in which I think such limitation must be frankly acknowledged. With all his "inward, sweet delight in God and in divine things," one cannot help feeling at times a certain strain in the piety of Edwards, as if he were bent on disciplining himself to live at a height of religious emotion which it does not lie in the weakness of human nature to sustain. There is a tension as of the over-bent bow in much of his experience, resulting, as his *Diary* faithfully shows, in painful fluctuations of feeling — alternations of periods of rapture with seasons of depression — begetting in himself the suspicion, as he says, that "too constant a mortification, and too vigorous an application to religion, may be prejudicial to health."

He puts himself under severe regimen; talks often of the need of "forcing" himself upon religious thoughts; drills himself with maxims in a way that reminds one of Marcus Aurelius; intends, at one point, to "live in a continual mortification," though his good sense led him afterwards to think better of it. This strained, introspective mood is not healthy, though it was characteristic of a good deal of the piety of the period, and of the times of "attention to religion," as revival-seasons were named.

Connected with this is the second limitation I would notice in Edwards. The intensity of his nature on the side of religion — absorbing, dwarfing all other interests — was not without an effect in limiting the range of his human sympathies. There is a lack of the humanist element in him; a defect in the appreciation of art, literature and culture, which was bound again to provoke, and did provoke a reaction. There is a lack also of full sympathy with human nature in the individual. The terrible intensity of his sense of the sovereignty of God, of the awfulness of sin, of the utter ruin wrought by sin — even with all that existed to balance it in his views of the love of God, and of the beauty and excellency of God and Christ — threw other truths out of proportion. There is a pitilessness sometimes in his delineations of the divine justice which amazes us. I suppose there are few more terrible pages in literature than those of some of Jonathan Edwards's sermons on the punishment of the lost. But let us do justice to our author even here. I do not know what the judgment of anyone of us would be on sin, or on ourselves as sinners, if we realized as we should do, or as it was given to him to do, the holiness of God. To him it was all most real. If we want to see how far it is possible for one to go in judgment of the damnableness of sin, who sees it in that light, we may recall Dante, who surpasses even Edwards in his lurid realism and intensity.

We dare not dismiss this as pure mediaevalism. The fact that Dante's *Inferno* has for many today all the fascination of a great classic, embodying lessons of eternal import, is a proof that his hell is not altogether an arbitrary, barbarous, and exploded conception. Still in Dante's pictures of the circles there is a touch of sympathy — a sense of gradations — which there is not in Edwards. One asks in vain where the "few stripes" and "many stripes" come in with him. But neither Dante nor Edwards in their representations of the future can be held to do justice to the possibilities of grace in the Gospel. Not nature only, but grace, rises in rebellion in us at these merciless descriptions, and says — " There must be something more, something else," though it may not be possible to tell precisely what it is, and though many, in attempting to define it, have been wise above what is written. If these descriptions by either Dante or Edwards could be presumed to be the last words on the subject, I think we should have to go back to Dr. Walter Smith's picture in his poem on "The Self-Exiled,"

> "The meek soul that for love heeds not what sorrow befalls it,
> Heeds not the bliss and the glory, but longs for them that are lying
> Dim in the outer darkness, tossed in the anguish undying"

and which, amidst angelic silence, pleads for permission

> " To go away,
> And help, if I yet may help, the dead
> That have no day."

I do not think however that we are shut up to this conclusion either.

I should like in closing to recall that Scotland also may claim its little share of influence on the influence of Edwards. Probably nothing in the course of his own life ever impressed Jonathan Edwards more deeply than his brief association with David Brainerd. It is worth remembering therefore that when Brainerd went to the Indians, it was as a missionary of the Society in Scotland for Propagating Christian Knowledge. Further, it was through his Life of Brainerd that Edwards produced some of his deepest impressions on individual minds. It is said that the reading of the work had a potent influence on the mind of Carey, of Henry Martyn, and of the saintly McCheyne in Scotland. If so, in the last case, Edwards was but giving back to Scotland what was in part given by it.

APPENDICES

APPENDIX I.

INTRODUCTORY.

Edwards began in his college days, apparently, four series of papers. The first he entitles, "The Natural History of the Mental World, or of the Internal World: being a Particular Enquiry into the Nature of the Human Mind, with respect to both its Faculties — the Understanding and the Will, — and its various Instincts, and Active and Passive Powers." A briefer title is "The Mind." The second series is referred to by its author as "Natural Philosophy," and as dealing with the "External World." Dr. Dwight designates it "Notes on Science." The third, Edwards calls "Miscellanies." The fourth he often refers to as containing a "Note" on this or that passage of Scripture. Most of this collection was published by Dr. Dwight under the title "Notes on the Bible." "The Mind" and the "Natural Philosophy" are to be found in the Appendix to the first volume of Dwight's edition of Edwards's "Works." The autographs of the papers on the "External World," are in my possession; those on the "Mental World" have strangely disappeared. The originals of the "Miscellanies" and the Scriptural "Notes" are deposited in the Library of Yale University, and I am much indebted to Professor Franklin Bowditch Dexter, for opportunities and kind assistance in the examination of these and other autographs, of which he has given an interesting account in a communication published in the "Proceedings of the Massachusetts Historical Society, March, 1901." The remarks on topics in Natural and Mental Philosophy seem to have been discontinued after their author was ordained, early in 1727, as a minister of the Gospel in

APPENDIX I.

Northampton. His first biographer, however, a pupil and intimate friend, testifies not only that he "had an uncommon taste for Natural Philosophy," but that he "cultivated" it "to the end of his life, with that justness and accuracy of thought which was almost peculiar to him." I have noticed in the rich collection at New Haven, a loose sheet, on which characteristic questions relating to both scientific and philosophical problems are noted in a hand-writing which suggests maturity. Yet it remains true that the only series which were continuously prosecuted through his life were those which dealt with Biblical and theological themes. The number of topics entered in the "Miscellanies" increased to 1408. They are contained, says Professor Dexter, "in eight folio or quarto volumes, aggregating over 1,400 minutely written pages." From this repository of his thoughts were drawn the contents of two volumes published in Edinburgh from copies supplied by the younger President Edwards, and a third collection was added to these by Dr. Dwight, and is to be found in the eighth volume of his edition of the "Works." Professor Dexter says that what has thus been used is "only a fragment of the whole amount." Of numbers in this collection, not included in any edition of Edwards's "Works," I have copies written by an amanuensis employed by Dr. Sereno E. Dwight, and revised by him. These, together with others made for the son, Dr. Jonathan Edwards, amount to more than 1700 full pages, allowing ten and one-half inches by eight and one-half inches for each page. The hand-writing of Dr. Dwight's scribe is large, and plain as print, so that by these transcripts the study is greatly facilitated of a collection of which Professor Dexter remarks: "No representation of Edwards as a thinker is quite complete so long as so

APPENDIX I.

many of these 'Miscellanies' are still in manuscript." Perhaps some misunderstandings of his theology, or apologetic suggestions which appear to have somewhat misled, would not have appeared, had the perusal of these papers not been so peculiarly difficult.

They are far from being all of special interest or value. Some are mere references to authors, or to Edwards's own Notes on passages of Scriptures. Others are brief remarks or conclusions. Only a minor part are extended discussions. A fair idea of their varying length may be gained from the "Notes on the Bible" published by Dr. Dwight, who gives the number of each selection which he uses.

It should be added, that the descriptive phrases "Note-book," "Common-place book," often applied to the "Miscellanies," though not, as already implied, wholly erroneous, may easily mislead. Especially inapplicable is the word "tentative." The *Observations* make a strong impression of being the results of protracted thought that had reached careful conclusions and results which they were intended to preserve. Progress in reflection is observable. The earlier papers should be compared with later ones on the same themes. Justice to their author requires that they be regarded as written primarily for his own eye, and as helps in the prosecution of his ever unwearied efforts in the attainment and maintenance of truth. But "tentative" they are not, in the sense of something merely set down for further consideration, and with a reserve of more or less doubt as to its validity. Samuel Hopkins, the younger Edwards, and Dr. Dwight, as already noticed, have drawn freely from these "Miscellanies;" and we have their author's own testimony as to their relation to his opinions and judgments, as will be evident by the following extract from his letter

APPENDIX I.

to the Trustees of Nassau Hall, who had chosen him to its presidency: "My method of study, from my first beginning the work of the ministry, has been very much by writing; applying myself, in this way, to improve every important hint; pursuing the clue to my utmost, when anything in reading, meditation, or conversation, has been suggested to my mind, that seemed to promise light, in any weighty point; thus penning what appeared to me my best thoughts, on innumerable subjects, for my own benefit."[1] "Best thoughts" would be a not inapt description of the contents of the "Miscellanies" as a whole.

The quotations included in this Appendix relate to remarks made in the Address on the "Theology of Jonathan Edwards,"[2] and are intended to illustrate and justify them. They show the life-long presence in Edwards's mind of the thoughts expressed, and also, so far as this occurred, their growth. I wish particularly to remove a suspicion which recently has gained more or less currency, — (reversing rather curiously a former supposition) — that Edwards's interest in the doctrine of the Trinity was of late origin, and that it arose, in part at least, from a distrust in his mind of the validity of his own theological system. In the selections from the *Observations* on the "End of God in the Creation" I desire especially to indicate what a complete and beautiful unity is disclosed between his highest and long cherished thought of God, and his conception of the Divine Purpose in Creation, a view essentially different, I may add, from either a deistic or a pantheistic interpretation of the universe.   E. C. S.

[1] Dwight's *Life* [*Works*, Vol. I. p. 569].
[2] See above, p. 73.

APPENDIX I.

A. THE TRINITY.

Before proceeding with citations from the "Miscellanies," I will introduce a few sentences from the *first* and *forty-fifth* numbers on "The Mind," since these papers are not published in the edition of Edwards's Works in common use. No. 1 was probably written before he began his "Miscellanies," and No. 45 is earlier apparently than anything on the Trinity in the theological series.

"1. *Excellency.* This is an universal definition of Excellency: *The Consent of Being to Being*, or *Being's Consent to Entity.* . . . . One alone, without any reference to any more, cannot be excellent, for in such case there can be no manner of relation no way, and therefore no such thing as consent. Indeed, what we call *One* may be excellent because of a consent of parts, or some consent of those in that being that are distinguished into a plurality some way or other. But in a being that is absolutely without any plurality, there cannot be Excellency, for there can be no such thing as consent or agreement."

"45. *Excellence.* When we spake of Excellence in Bodies we were obliged to borrow the word, *Consent*, from Spiritual things; but Excellence in and among Spirits is in its prime and proper sense, Being's consent to Being. There is no other proper consent but that of *Minds*, even of their Will; which, when it is of Minds towards Minds, it is *Love*, and when of Minds towards other things it is *Choice*. Wherefore all the Primary and Original beauty or excellence that is among Minds is Love; and into this may all be resolved that is found among them. . . . . His [God's] Infinite Beauty is His Infinite mutual Love of Himself . . . . the mutual love of the Father and the Son. This makes the Third, the Personal Holy Spirit, or the Holiness of God, which is

APPENDIX I.

his Infinite Beauty. . . . . 'Tis peculiar to God, that he has beauty *within himself*, consisting in Being's consenting with his own Being, or the love of himself, in his own Holy Spirit. . . . . We shall be in danger, when we meditate on this love of God to himself as being the thing wherein his infinite excellence and loveliness consists, of some alloy to the sweetness of our view, by its appearing with something of the aspect and cast of what we call self-love. But we are to consider that this love includes in it, or rather is the same as, a love to everything, as they are all communications of himself. So that we are to conceive of Divine Excellence as the Infinite General Love, that which reaches all proportionally with perfect purity and sweetness; yea, it includes the true Love of all creatures, for that is his Spirit, or which is the same thing, his Love."

The following citations are all from the "Miscellanies." They are taken from the collections of copies prepared for Dr. Dwight in connection with his edition of Edwards's works. They have been carefully compared with the originals, and in spelling and capitalization more closely conformed to those.

"94.[1] *Trinity.* There has been much cry of late against saying one word particularly about the Trinity, but what the Scripture has said, judging it impossible but that, if we did, we should err in a thing so much above us. But if they call that, which necessarily results from the putting of reason and Scripture [together] though it has not been said in Scripture in express words, I say if they call this what is not said in the Scriptures, I am not afraid to say twenty things about the Trinity,

---

[1] Forty-eight should be added to each number cited from the "Miscellanies," as before explained. Dr. Dwight supposes that 150 of the *Observations* were written during Edwards's college days and the two years following his graduation.

APPENDIX I.

which the Scriptures never said. There may be deductions of reason from what has been said of the most mysterious matters, besides what has been said, and safe and certain deductions too, as well as about the most obvious and easy matters.

I think that it is within the reach of naked reason to perceive certainly that there are thus, distinct, in God, each of which is the same, three that must be distinct, and that there are not, nor can be any more, distinct, Really and truly distinct, but three, either distinct persons or properties, or anything else; and that, of these three one is (more properly than any thing else) begotten of the other, and that the other Proceeds alike from both, and that the first neither is begotten nor proceeds. It is often said that God is infinitely happy from all eternity, in the view and enjoyment of himself, in the reflection and inverse love of his own essence that is in the infinitely perfect idea he has of himself infinitely perfect. The Almighty's knowledge is not so different from ours, but that ours is the image of it; is by an idea as ours is only 'tis infinitely Perfect; if it were not by idea it is in no respect like ours : 'tis not what we call knowledge, nor anything whereof knowledge is the resemblance; for the whole of human knowledge, both in the beginning and end of it, consists in ideas. 'Tis also said that God's knowledge of himself includes the knowledge of all things, and that he knows, and from eternity knew, all things, by the looking on himself, and by the idea of himself, because he is virtually all things: so that all God's knowledge is the idea of himself. But yet it would suppose imperfection in God, to suppose that God's idea of himself is anything different from himself. None will suppose that God has any such ideas as we, that are only as it were the shadow of things, and not the very things.

APPENDIX I.

We cannot suppose that God reflects on himself after the imperfect manner we reflect on things, for we can view nothing immediately. The immediate object of the mind's intuition is the idea alwaies and the soul receives nothing but ideas. But God's intuition on himself without doubt is immediate. But 'tis certain it cannot be except his idea be his essence, for his idea is the immediate object of his intuition. An absolutely perfect idea of a thing, is the very thing, for it wants nothing that is in the thing; substance, nor nothing else. That is the notion of the perfection of an idea, to want nothing that is in [shorthand]. Whatsoever is perfectly and absolutely like a thing, is that thing; but God's idea is absolutely perfect. I will form my reasoning thus: If nothing has any existence any way at all but in some consciousness or idea or other, and therefore that things, that are in us created consciousness, have no existence but in the divine idea[1] . . . . Supposing the things in this room were in the idea of none but of God, they would have existence no other way; and if the things in this Room would nevertheless be Real things; then God's idea, being a perfect idea, is Really the thing itself; and if so, and all God's ideas are only the one idea of himself, as has been shewn, [then God's idea] must be his Essence itself, it must be a substantial idea, having all the perfection of the substance perfectly; so that by God's reflecting on himself the Deity is begotten: there is a substantial image of God begotten, I am satisfied that though this word begotten had never been used in Scripture, it would have been used in this case; there is no other word that so properly expresses it. It is this perfection of God's idea that makes all things truly

---

[1] After the word "idea" Edwards wrote "as we have shown in Philosophy our natural [?] Philosophy," and drew a line through these words.

APPENDIX I.

and Properly present to him from all eternity; and is the reason why God has no succession. For every thing that is, has been, or shall be, having been perfectly in God's idea from all eternity; and a perfect Idea (which yet no finite being can have of anything) being the very thing; therfore all things from eternity were equally Present with God, and there is no alteration made in idea by presence and absence, as there is in us.

Again: That which is the express and perfect image of God, is God's idea of his own essence. There is nothing else can be an express, and fully perfect image of God but God's idea. Ideas are images of things and there are no other images of things, in the most proper sense, but ideas; because other things are only called images, as they beget an idea in us of the thing of which they are the image; so that all other images of things are but images in a secondary sense. But we know that the Son of God is the Express and Perfect image of God, and his image in the primary and most proper sense: II. Cor. iv. 4; Philip. ii. 6; Coloss. i. 15; Heb. i. 3.

Again: That Image of God which God infinitely loves, and has his chief delight in, is the Perfect idea of God. It has always been said that God's infinite delight consists in reflecting on himself and viewing his own perfections; or, which is the same thing, in his own perfect idea of himself; so that 'tis acknowledged that God's infinite love is to, and his infinite delight in, the perfect image of himself. But the Scriptures tell us that the Son of God is that Image of God which he infinitely loves. Nobody will deny this, that God infinitely loves his Son, John iii. 35; v. 20. So it was declared from heaven by the Father at his baptism and transfiguration, "This is my beloved Son, in whom I am well pleased." So the Father calls him his Elect in whom his soul delighteth,

APPENDIX I.

Isai. xlii. 1. He is called "the Beloved," Ephes. i. 6. The Son also declared that the Father's infinite happiness consisted in the enjoyment of him, Prov. viii. 30. Now none I suppose will say that God enjoys infinite happiness in two manners: one in the infinite delight he has in enjoying his Son, his Image; and another in the view of himself different from this. If not, then these ways, wherein God enjoys infinite happiness, are both the same; that is, his infinite delight in the idea of himself is the same with the infinite delight he has in his son: and if so, his Son and the idea he has of himself are the same.

Again: That, which is the Express Image of God, in which God enjoys infinite happiness, and is also the Word of God, is God's perfect idea of God. The Word of God, in its most proper meaning, is a transcript of the divine perfections: this Word is either his declared word of God or the essential [Word]. The one is the copy of the divine perfections given to us; the other is the perfect transcript thereof in God's own mind. But the perfect transcript of the perfections of God in the divine [mind] is the same with God's perfect idea of his own perfections. But I need tell none how the Son of God is called the Word of God.

Nextly: That which is the Express Image of God, in which is his infinite delight, which is his Word, and which is the Reason, or Wisdom of God, is God's perfect Idea of God. That God's knowledge, or reason, or wisdom, is the same with God's idea, none will deny; and that all God's knowledge or wisdom consists in the knowledge, or perfect idea, of himself, is shewn before, and granted by all; but none need to be told that the Son of God is often called in Scripture by the names of the Wisdom and Logos of God. Wherefore God himself has put the matter beyond all debate whether or no

APPENDIX I.

his Son is not the same with his Idea of himself; for it is most certain that his wisdom and knowledge is the very same with his idea of himself. How much does the Son of God speak in Proverbs under the name of Wisdom!

There is very much of image of this in ourselves. Man is as if he were two, as some of the great wits of this age have observed; a sort of genius is with man, that accompanies him and attends wherever he goes, so that a man has a conversation with himself, that is, he has a conversation with his own idea; so that, if his idea be excellent, he will take great delight and happiness in conferring and communicating with it: he takes complacency in himself, he applauds himself; and wicked men accuse them and fight with themselves, as if they were two; and man is truly happy then, and only then, when these two agree, and they delight in themselves, and in their own idea, their image, as God delights in his.

The Holy Spirit is the Act of God, between the Father and the Son infinitely loving and delighting in each other. Sure I am that, if the Father and the Son do infinitely delight in each other, there must be an infinitely pure and perfect Act between them, an infinitely sweet energy, which we call delight: This is certainly distinct from the other two. The delight and energy that is begotten in us by an idea, is distinct from the idea; so it cannot be confounded in God; either with God begetting or with his idea and image, or Son. It is distinct from each of the other two; and yet it is God: for the pure and perfect Act of God is God, because God is a pure Act. It appears that this is God, because that which acts perfectly, is all act, and nothing but act. There is image of this in created beings that approach to perfect action; how frequently do we say that the saints of heaven are all transformed into love, dissolved into joy, become activity itself, changed into pure extasy. I acknowledge these are metaphorical in this case; but yet it is true that the more perfect the act is, the more it resembles the infinitely perfect act of God in this respect. And I believe it will be plain to one that thinks intensely, that the perfect act of God must be a substantial act. We say that the perfect delights of reasonable creatures are substantial delights; but the delight of God is properly a substance, yea, an infinitely perfect substance, even the essence of God. It appears, by the holy Scriptures, that the holy Spirit is the perfect act of God. The name declares it, the Spirit of God denotes to us the activity, vivacity, and energy of God; and it appears that the holy Spirit is the pure act of God, and energy of the Deity of his office, which is to actuate and quicken all things, and to beget energy and vivacity in the creature; and it also appears that the holy Spirit is this act of the Deity, even love and delight, because from eternity there was no other act in God but thus acting with respect to himself, and delighting perfectly and infinitely in himself, or that infinite delight there is between the Father and the Son, for the object of God's perfect act must necessarily be himself, because there is no other. But we have shown that the Object of the divine mind is God's Son and Idea; and what other act can be thought of in God from eternity, but delighting in himself, the act of love which God is, I. John iv. 8. And if God is Love, and he that dwelleth in love dwelleth in God, and God in him, doubtless this intends principally the infinite love God has to himself. So that the scripture has implicitly told us that that love, which is between the Father and the Son, is God. The Holy Spirit's name is the Comforter, but no doubt but 'tis the infinite delight God has in himself, in the Comforter, that is the fountain of all delight and comfort.

APPENDIX 1.

It may be objected that at this rate one may prove an infinite number of persons in the godhead, for each person has an idea of the other person, thus the Father may have an idea of his Son, but you will argue that his idea must be substantial. I answer, that the Son himself is the Father's idea, himself : and if he has an idea of this idea, it is yet the same idea, a perfect idea of an idea is the same idea still to all intents and purposes.

Thus, when I have a perfect idea of my idea of an equilateral triangle, it is an idea of the same equilateral triangle to all intents and purposes. So if you say that God the Father or Son, may have an idea of their own delight in each other ; but I say a perfect idea or perception of one's own perfect delight cannot be different, at least in God, from the delight itself. You'll say the Son has an idea of the Father, I answer the Son himself is the idea of the Father, and if you say he has an idea of the Father, his idea is still an idea of the Father, and therefore the same with the Son ; and if you say the Holy Spirit has an idea of the father, I answer the Holy Spirit is himself the delight and joyfulness of the Father in that Idea and of the Idea in the Father. 'Tis still the Idea of the Father ; so that if we turn it all the ways in the world, we shall never be able to make more than these three : God, the idea of God, and delight in God.

I think it really evident from the light of reason that there are those three, distinct in God. If God has an idea of himself there is really a Duplicity, because [if] there is no duplicity it will follow that Jehovah thinks of himself no more than a stone ; and if God loves himself, and delights in himself, there is really a Triplicity, Three that cannot be confounded ; each of which are the Deity substantially.

And this is the only distinction that can be found or

APPENDIX I.

thought of in God. If it shall be said that there are power, wisdom, goodness, and holiness, in God, and that these may as well be proved to be distinct persons, because everything that is in God is God; [I answer,] as to the Power of God, Power always consists in something; the power of the mind consists in its wisdom, the power of the body in plenty of animal spirits and toughness of limbs, etc. And as it is distinct from those other things tis only a relation of adequateness and sufficiency of the essense to everything. But if we distinguish it from relation, it is nothing else but the essense of God, and if we take it for that where is that by which God exerts himself, it is no other than the Father; for the perfect energy of God with respect to himself is the most proper exertion of himself, of which the creation of the world is but a shadow. As to the Wisdom of God, we have already observed that this wholly consists in God's idea of himself, and is the same with the Son of God. And as to Goodness, the eternal exertion of the essense of that attribute, it is nothing but infinite Love, which, the Apostle John says, is God; and as we have observed that all divine love may be resolved into God's infinite love to himself, therefore this attribute, as it was exerted from eternity, is nothing but the Holy Spirit, which is exactly agreeable to the notion some have had of the Trinity. And as to holiness, tis delight in excellency; tis God's truest consent to himself, or in other words his perfect delight in himself, which we have shewn to be the Holy Spirit."

"96. *Trinity*. The argument of this *Observation* is from the perfect goodness of God. I quote a few sentences.

"It appears that there must be more than a Unity in infinite and eternal Essence; otherwise the Goodness of

APPENDIX I.

God Can have no perfect exercises. To be Perfectly Good, is to incline to, and delight in, making another happy in the same proportion as it is happy itself: that is, it delights as much in communicating happiness to another as in enjoying it himself, and [is] an inclination to communicate all his happiness. . . . . God must have a perfect Exercise of his Goodness, and therefore must have the fellowship of a person equal with himself."

"98. *Trinity.*" This *Observation* finds in the Biblical application to the Holy Spirit of the Symbol of a Dove reason for supposing that He " is nothing but the infinite love and delight of God." Part of p. 103 of the "Essay" recently published by Professor Fisher is identical with this number. The closing sentence of the *Observation* is clearer than the corresponding one in the "Essay." It reads: "It was under this representation that the Holy [Ghost] descended on Christ at his Baptism, signifying the infinite love of the Father to the Son, and that thereby is signified that infinite love that is between the Father and the Son; which is further illustrated by the voice which came with the dove, 'This is my beloved Son, in whom I am well Pleased.'"

"117. *Trinity.* Love is certainly the Perfection as well as Happiness of a Spirit; God, doubtless, as he is infinitely Perfect and happy, has infinite love. I cannot doubt but that God loves infinitely, properly speaking, and not with that which some Call self-love, whereby even the devils desire pleasure, and are averse to pain, which is exceeding improperly called love; and is nothing at all akin to that affection or delight, which is called love. Then there must have been an object from all Eternity, which God infinitely loves. But we have shewed that all love arises from the perception, either of Consent to being in General, or Consent to that being that percieves.

APPENDIX I.

Infinite loveliness, to God, therefore must consist either in infinite Consent to Entity in General, or infinite consent to God. But we have shewn that consent to Entity, and consent to God are the same, because God is the General and only proper Entity of all things; so that it is necessary that that object which God infinitely loves must be infinitely and perfectly consenting and agreeable to him; but that which infinitely and perfectly agrees is the very same essense, for if it be different it dont infinitely consent."

"133. *Trinity.* Coroll. to a former meditation of the trinity. hence we see how Generation by the Father, and yet Coetaneity with the Father, or being begotten, and yet being eternal, are Consistent; for it is Easy to Concieve how this image, this thought, Reason or Wisdom of God should be eternally Begotten by him, and begotten by him from Eternity, and Continually through Eternity. And so the holy Spirit, that personal Energy, the divine love and delight, Eternally and Continually proceeds from both.

"Coroll. 2. Hence we see how and in what sense the Father is the fountain of the Godhead, and how naturally and Properly God the Father is spoken of in scripture, as of the Deity without distinction, as being the only True God, and why God the Son should [be] commonly spoken of with a distinction, and be called the Son of God; and so the holy Spirit, the Spirit of God. ☞ Remember to Look, the next time I have the opportunity of, to see if Spirit, in scripture Phrase, is not Commonly put for affection, and never for understanding; and to shew that there is no other affection in God but love to himself."

"136. *Trinity.* The word Spirit most Commonly in Scripture is put for affections of the mind; but there is

APPENDIX I.

no other affection in God essentially, properly, and primarily, but love and delight, and that in himself; for into this is his love and delight in his Creatures resolvable.

"I dont Remember that any other attributes are said to be God, and God to be them but λόγος and, ἀγάπη, or *Reason* and *love*. I Conclude because no other are in that (a personal) sense." . . . . . .

"141. *Trinity*. vid. I believe that Jesus Christ not only is exactly *in* the image of [God], but in the most proper sense *is* the image of God. Now however exactly one being, suppose of one human body, [may be] like another, Yet I think one is not in the most proper sense the image of the other, but more Properly in the image of the other. Adam did not beget a son that was his image properly, but *in* his image; but the idea of a thing is, in the most proper sense of all, its image; and God's idea the most perfect image." . . . . . .

"150. *Deity*. Many have wrong conceptions of the difference between the nature of the Deity and that of Created spirits. The difference is no contrariety, but what naturally Results from his Greatness and nothing else; such as Created spirits come nearer to, or more imitate, the Greater they are in their Powers and faculties. So that if we should suppose the faculties of a Created spirit to be enlarged infinitely, there would be the Deity to all intents and Purposes: the same simplicity, immutability, etc."

"179. *Logos*. It the more Confirms me in it that the Perfect Idea, God has of himself, is truly and Properly God, that the existence of all Corporeal things is only Ideas."[1]

---

[1] Edwards's idealism is not subjective. See *Am. Journal of Theology*, 1897, p. 959; *Jonathan Edwards' Idealisms: Inaugural Dissertation* . . . . von John Henry MacCracken, Ph.D., Halle A. S., C. A. Kaemmerer & Co., 1899; *The Early Idealism of Edwards*, by Prof.

APPENDIX I.

"184. *Union. Spiritual.* [From] What insight I have of the nature of minds I am convinced that there is no Guessing what kind of union and mixtion by Consciousness, or otherwise, there may be between them; so that all difficulty is Removed in believing what the scripture declares about spiritual union of the Persons of the Trinity, of the two natures of Christ, of Christ and the minds of Saints."

"194. *God.* That is a Gross and unprofitable idea we have of God, as being something Large and Gross as bodies are, and infinitely extended throughout the immense Space: For God is neither little, nor Great, with that sort of Greatness: even as the Soul of man is not at all extended, no more than an idea, and is not present anywhere as bodies are present as we have shewn elsewhere. So t'is with respect to the uncreated Spirit. The Greatness of a Soul Consists not in any extension but [in] its comprehensiveness of Idea and extendedness of operation. So the infiniteness of God Consists in his perfect Comprehension of all things, and the extendedness of his operation equally to all Places. . . . We ought to concieve of God as being omnipotence, perfect knowledge and Perfect Love; . . . . and not as if it was a sort of unknown thing, that we Call substance, that is extended."

"238. *Trinity.* Those Ideas which we Call Ideas of

H. Norman Gardiner, A. M., republished in *Jonathan Edwards: A Retrospect*, Houghton, Mifflin & Co., 1901.

I noticed on a loose leaf, in the New Haven Collection of Edwards's *Mss.*, apparently in a later hand-writing than the early papers, this entry: "How there may be more in material Existence than Man's Perception, past, Present, or future.

"Show how far the Perception of superior spirits may belong to this [illegible] "and how far the Perception of God."

Edwards's Idealism ("Spiritualism".) always includes a something "more" than subjectivism recognizes; viz. "a perfectly stable idea in God's mind, together with his stable Will . . . . with respect to corresponding communications to Created Minds, and effects on their minds;" or, as phrased on the leaf referred to above, "an universe of coexisting and successive Perceptions connected by such wonderful methods and Laws."

APPENDIX I.

Reflection, all Ideas of the acts of the mind, such as the Idea of thought, of Choice, love, fear, etc., if we diligently attend to our own minds we shall find, they are not properly Representations, but are indeed Repetitions of those very things, either more fully, or more faintly; they therefore are not properly Ideas. Thus, t' is impossible to have an Idea of thought, or of an Idea, but it will [be] that same Idea Repeated. So if we think of love, either of our past love that is now vanished, or of the love of others which we have not, we either so frame things in our Imagination that we have for a moment a love to that thing, or to something we make represent it, or we excite for a moment that love which we have, and suppose it in another place, or we have only an idea of the Antecedents, Concomitants, and effects of love, and suppose something unseen, and Govern our thoughts about as we have learned how by experience and habit. Let any one try himself in a particular instance, and diligently observe. So if we have an Idea of a Judgment not our own, we have the same Ideas, that are the terms of the Proposition, Repeated in our own minds, and recur to something in our own minds, that is Really our Judgment, and suppose it there, [That is we Govern our thoughts about it as if it were there]. if we have a distinct Idea of that Judgment; or else we have only an Idea of the attendants and effects of the Judgment, and supply the name, and our actions about it as we have habituated ourselves. And so Certainly it is in all our spiritual Ideas; they are the very same things Repeated perhaps very faintly and obscurely, and very quick, and momentaneously, and with many new References, suppositions, and translations. But if the Idea be perfect, it is only the same thing absolutely over again.

Now if this be certain, as it seems to me to be, then its

quite Clear that if God doth think of himself, and understand himself with perfect Clearness, fulness, and distinctness, that that Idea he hath of himself is absolutely himself, again, and is God perfectly to all Intents and purposes. That [idea] which God hath of the divine nature and Essence is really and fully the divine nature and Essence again. So that by God's thinking of himself, the Deity must certainly be Generated, this seems exceedingly Clear to me.

God doubtless understands himself in the most proper sense, for therein his infinite understanding chiefly consists; and he understands himself at all times perfectly, without intermission or succession in his thoughts.

When we have the Idea of another's love to a thing, if it be the love of a man to a woman that we are unconcerned about; in such cases we have not generally any proper Idea at all of his Love, we only have an Idea of his actions that are the effects of love, as we have found by experience, and of those external things which belong to Love, and which appear in Case of Love; or if we have any Idea of it, it is either by forming our Ideas so of persons and things as we suppose they appear to them, that we have a faint vanishing motion of their affection; or, if the thing be a thing that we so hate, that this can't be, we have our love to something else faintly and least excited, and so in the mind as it were referred to this place, we think this is Like that."

" 259. *Trinity*. T' is Evident that there are no more than these three Really distinct in God : God, and his Idea, and his Love or Delight. We cant concieve of any further Real distinctions. If you say there is the Power of God ; I answer, the Power of a being, even in Creatures is nothing distinct from the being itself besides a mere Relation to an effect. If you say there is the

APPENDIX I.

Infiniteness, Eternity, and Immutability of God; they are mere modes and manners of existence. If you say there is the wisdom of God; that is the Idea of God. If you say there is the holiness of God; that is not different from his Love as we have shewn, and is the holy Spirit. If you say there is the Goodness and mercy of God; they are included in his Love, they are his Love with a Relation. We Can find no more in God, that even in Creatures are distinct from the very being; or, there is no more than those three in God, but what even in Creatures are only but the same with the very being, or only some mere modes, or Relations, duration, extension, Changeableness, or unchangeableness, so far as attributed to Creatures, or only mere modes, and Relations of existence. There are no more than these three that are distinct in God, even in our way of concieving.

There is in Resemblance to this threefold distinction in God a threefold distinction in a Created Spirit: namely, the spirit itself, and its understanding, and its will, or Inclination, or love; and this Indeed is all the real distinction there is in Created spirits."

"260. *Trinity*. There is no other properly Spiritual Image but Idea, although there may be another Spiritual thing that is exactly like. Yet one thing being exactly like another dont make it the proper image of that thing. If there be any distinct spiritual substance exactly like another, yet is not the proper image of the other, tho one be made after the other, yet it is not any more an Image of the first, than the first is of the Last.

That Christ is the spiritual Image and Idea of God see John xii. 45; xiv. 7, 8, 9. Seeing the Perfect Idea of a thing, is, to all Intents and purposes, the same as seeing the thing. It is not only equivalent to seeing of it, but it

APPENDIX I.

is seeing of it; for there is no other seeing but having an Idea. Now, by seeing a perfect Idea, so far as we see it, we have it. But it cant be said of anything else, that, in seeing of it, we see another, speaking strictly, except it be the very Idea of the other. The Oil, that signifies the Holy Ghost, with which Christ is anointed, is Called the oil of gladness: the Holy Ghost is God's delight, joy. Ps. xlv. 7, Isai. lxi. 3. "The oil of joy for mourning." They anointed themselves to express Joy.

Another Name of the Son of God that shows that he is God's perfect Idea, is the Amen, which is a Hebrew word that signifies truth. Divine truth, or the Eternal truth of God, is God's perfect understanding of himself, which is his perfect understanding of all things."

"308. *Trinity.* With Respect to that Objection against this explication of the Trinity, that according to the truth of this Reasoning there would not only be three persons, but an Infinite number, for we must suppose that the Son understands the Father, as well as the Father the son, and Consequently the Son has an Idea of the father and so that Idea will be another person, and so may be said of the Holy Ghost: This objection is but a colour without substance, and arises in a Confusion of thought and a misunderstanding of what we say. In the first place we dont suppose that the Father, the Son, and the Holy Ghost, are three distinct beings, that have three distinct understandings. It is the Divine essense that understands, and it is the divine essence is understood; Tis the Divine being that loves, and tis the Divine being that is loved. The father understands, the Son understands, and the holy Ghost understands, because every one is the same understanding Divine essense and not that Each of them had a distinct understanding of their own. 2. We never supposed the Father gene-

APPENDIX I.

rated the Son by Understanding the Son; but that God Generated the Son by understanding his own Essense, and that the Son is that Idea itself, or Understanding of the Essense. The Father understands the Son, no otherwise than as he understands that essence, that is the essence of the Son. The Father understands the Idea he has merely in his having that Idea without any other act: thus a man understands his own perfect Idea, merely by his having that Idea in his mind. So the Son understands the Father in that the Essense of the Son understands the essence of the Father, or in himself being the understanding of that Essense, and so of the holy Ghost. After you have In your imagination multiplied understandings and loves never so often, it will be the Understanding and loving the very same essense, and you can never make more than these three; God, and the Idea of God, and the love of God. But I would not be understood to pretend to Give a full explication of the Trinity; for I think it still remains an Incomprehensible mystery, the Greatest and the most Glorious of all mysteries."

"309. *Trinity*. The name of the Second person in the Trinity, Λογος, evidences that he is God's Idea; whether we translate the word *the Reason* of God, or *the word* of God. If the *Reason* or the *Understanding* of God, the matter is past Dispute; for everyone will own that the Reason or understanding of God is his Idea. And if we translate it the word of God, he is either the outward word of God or his Inward. None will say he is his outward. Now the outward word is Speech; but the inward word, which is the Original of it, is thought, the Scripture being its own Interpreter; for how often is thinking in Scripture called *Speaking*, when applied to God and men: So that it is the Idea, if we take the Scripture for our Guide, that is the Inward word."

APPENDIX I.

"330. *Holy Ghost.* It appears that the holy Spirit is the holiness or excellency and delight of God, because our Communion with God, and with Christ, Consists in our Partaking of the holy Ghost: II. Cor. xiii. 14; I. Cor. vi. 17; I. John iii. 24; and iv. 13. The Oil that was upon Aaron's head Ran Down to the Skirts of his Garments. The Spirit, which Christ, our head, has without measure, is Communicated to his Church and people. The sweet Perfumed oil signified Christ's excellency, and sweet delight. Philip. ii. 1.

Communion we know is nothing else but the Common partaking with others of good. Communion with God is nothing else but a partaking with him of his excellency, his holiness, and happiness."

"336. *Trinity.* All the metaphorical Representations of the holy Ghost in the Scripture, such as water, fire, breath, wind, oil, wine, a spring, a River of Living water as proceeding from God, do Abundantly the most Naturally Represent the perfectly active, flowing affection, Holy love and Pleasure of God. So the holy Ghost is said to be Poured out, and shed forth; Acts ii. 32, 33. Titus iii. 5, 6. So Love is said to be shed abroad in our hearts."

"341. *Trinity.* I can think of no other Good account that Can be Given of the apostle Paul's wishing Grace and peace, or Grace, mercy, and Peace from God the Father, and the Lord Jesus Christ in the beginning of his Epistles without Ever mentioning the holy Ghost, but that the holy Ghost is the Grace, the Love and peace of God the Father, and (the) Lord Jesus Christ. We find it so *fourteen times* in all his salutations, in the beginning of his Epistles; and, in his blessing at the end of his II Epistle to the Corinthians, where all three Persons are mentioned, he wishes *Grace* and *Love* from the Son and the Father, but *the Communion* of the holy Ghost, that is the *Partaking of him*. The blessing from the Father and the Son, is the holy Ghost; but the blessing from the holy Ghost is himself, a Communication of himself."

"362. *Trinity.* We have a lively Image of the Trinity in the Sun; The Father is as the substance of the sun; the Son is as the brightness and Glory of the disk of the sun, or that bright and Glorious form under which it appears to our eyes; the Holy Ghost is as the heat and Powerful influence, which acts upon the Sun itself, and being Diffusive Enlightens, warms, Enlivens, and comforts the world. The Spirit, as heat is God's Infinite Love and happiness, is as the Internal heat of the Sun; but, as it is that by which God communicates himself, he is as the Emitted beams of God's Glory: II. Cor. iii. 18, that is we are Changed to glory, or to a shining brightness, as Moses was, from, or by God's glory or shining, even as by the Spirit of the Lord, i. e. which Glory or shining is the spirit of the Lord. The word, that is translated From with Respect to Glory, and By with respect to the Spirit, is the same in the Original, it is απο, in both, and therefore would have been more intelligibly translated, "we are Changed By Glory into Glory, even as By the Spirit of the Lord." Moses was Changed by God's glory Shining upon him, even as we are Changed by God's Spirit, Shed as bright beams on us.

The Spirit of God is Called the Spirit of glory, 1 Peter iv. 14. The Spirit of glory Resteth upon you, upon two accounts, because it is the glory of God, and as it were his Emitted beams, and as it is the believer's glory, and causes him also to shine.

The various sorts of Rays of the Sun and their Beautiful Colours do well Represent the Spirit, and the amiable excellency of God, and the various beautiful

APPENDIX I.

Graces and virtues of the Spirit; the same we find in Scripture are made use of by God for that purpose, even to signify and Represent the Graces and virtues of the Spirit. Therefore I suppose the rainbow was Chosen to be a sign of the Covenant, and St. John saw a Rainbow Round about the throne of God, Rev. iv. 3, and a Rainbow upon the head of Christ, Chap. x. 1. So Ezekiel saw a Rainbow Round about the throne, Ezek. i. 28. And I believe the variety that there is in the Rays of the sun, and their various beautiful Colours were designed in the Creation for this very purpose. See Shadows of divine things, No. 58.

There is yet more of an Image of the Trinity in the soul of man. There is the mind, and its understanding or Idea, and the will or affection, or Love: answering to God, the Idea of God, and the love of God.

Indeed the whole animal Creation, which is but the shadows of beings, is So made as to Represent Spiritual things: it might be demonstrated by the wonderful agreement in thousands of things, much of the same kind as is between the types of the old testament and their antitypes; and by their being spiritual things — being so often and Continually compared with them in the word of God, and it is agreeable to God's wisdom that it should be so, that the Inferior and shadowy Parts of his works should be made to Represent those things that are more Real and excellent, spiritual and divine, to Represent the things that Immediately concern himself and the highest Parts of his work. Spiritual things are the Crown and glory, the head and soul, the very End and alpha, and Omega of all other works; what, therefore, can be more agreeable to wisdom than that they should be so made as to shadow them forth? and we know that this is according to God's method, which his wisdom has chosen in other matters.

APPENDIX I.

Thus the Inferiour Dispensation of the Gospel was all to shadow forth the highest and most excellent which was its end: thus almost Everything that was said or done, that we have Recorded in scripture from adam to Christ, was typical of Gospel things. Persons were typical persons; their actions were typical actions; the cities were typical cities; the nation of the Jews and other nations were typical nations; their Land was a typical Land; God's Providences towards them were typical Providences; their worship was typical worship; their houses were typical houses; their magistrates, typical magistrates; their clothes, typical clothes; and Indeed the world was a typical world. And this is God's manner to make inferior things shadows of the Superior, and most excellent; outward things shadows of spiritual; and all other things, shadows of those things that are the End of all things, and the Crown of all things. Thus God Glorifies himself and Instructs the minds that he has made."

"376. *Trinity*. It Can no other way be accounted for, that in the first of John i. 3, 'Our fellowship' is said to be 'with the Father, and with his Son Jesus Christ,' and that it is not said to be also with the holy Ghost, but because our Communion with them Consists in our Communion of the holy Ghost with them. It is in our Partaking of the holy Ghost, that we have Communion with Father and Son, and with Christians. This is the Common excellency and delight, in which they all are united: this is the bond of perfectness, by which they are one in the Father, and the Son, as the Father is in the Son and the Son in the Father."

"405. *Trinity*. It may be thus expressed, the Son is the Deity, Generated by God's understanding, or having an Idea of himself; the holy Ghost is the Divine Essence flowing out, or breathed forth in Infinite Love and Delight; or which is the same, the Son is God's Idea of himself, and the Spirit is God's Love to and delight In himself."

"446. *Trinity*. Christ is called the face of God, Exod. xxxiii, 14, and the angel of God's face, the word in the original signifies face, or looks, form, or appearance of a thing : Now what can be so fitly called so as God's own Perfect Idea of himself; whereby he has every moment a view of his own essence ? This is that face, aspect, form, or appearance, whereby God Eternally appears to himself, and more Perfectly than man appears to himself by his form or appearance in a looking glass. The Root, that the word comes from, signifies to look upon or behold. Now what is that which God looks upon, or beholds, in so Eminent a manner, as he doth on his own Idea, or the perfect Image of himself, which he has in view. This is that which is Eminently in his presence, this is the Angel of his presence".

"1065. *Trinity*. That the Spirit of God is the Love of God, well agrees to the Scripture names, appellations, and representations of this Person of the Trinity : his being called the Spirit of God, or *Breath* of God ; and being compared to water, to a Spring, a River, a Shower, to flowing oil, and precious ointment, to wind, and Fire ; and to his being represented as flowing forth, poured out, breathed forth, blowing, burning, being Quenched, etc. Holy affection is aptly compared to fire, to breath, to a flowing Stream, and is aptly spoken of as burning, being enkindled, cherished and quenched, flowing out, breathed forth, diffused abroad, etc. But the Representation would be very unnatural if we should speak of understanding, wisdom, or *Idea*, as breathed forth, poured out, shed abroad, burning, blowing, etc. And it is not very credible that those names, similitudes and Representa-

APPENDIX I.

tions that are given to the Holy Spirit, are no more adapted to him than to the other Persons of the Trinity, any other way than by an arbitrary constitution, or agreement of the Persons of the Trinity, appointing a Particular work to the Holy Spirit, no more suited to any thing in this person of the Trinity as he is in himself any more than to either of the other Persons, and that there was nothing in the nature of things but that the Son of God, or the Father might as properly have been appointed to the same office, and so that either of the former Persons of the Trinity, might in that Case as properly be Represented by breath, wind, Rain, a River, ointment and fire, and be spoken of as flowing, breathing forth, burning, shed abroad, being quenched, etc., as the Holy Spirit. I have shown No. 1062, Corol. that the second Person in the Trinity has not the name of the Son of God from his appointment to his office, and work on the affair of our Redemption; and there is no more Reason to think that the Spirit of God is so called only from his particular office and work in that affair."

"1162. It may be worthy of consideration whether or no some of the Heathen Philosophers had not with regard to some things, some degree of Inspiration of the Spirit of God, which led them to say such wonderful things concerning the Trinity, the Messiah, etc. Inspiration is not so high an Honor and Privilege as some are ready to think. It is no peculiar Privilege of God's Special favorites; many very bad men have been the subjects of it, yea some that were Idolaters. Balaam was an Idolater, and a great sorcerer, or wizard, and yet He was the subject of Inspiration, and that even when in the Practice of his witchcraft, when He went to seek by enchantments. Yea, the devils themselves, seem sometimes to have been immediately actuated by God, and forced to speak the Truth in Honor to Christ and his Religion. So the Devil at the oracle of Delphi was probably actuated by God, and compelled to confess Christ, and own that the Hebrew Child to be above him, and had sent Him to Hell, and forbidden Him to give forth any more oracles.

Why might not Socrates and Plato, and some others of the wise men of Greece have some degree of Inspiration; as well as the wise men from the East, who came to see Christ when an Infant. Those wise men dwelt among the Heathen, as much as the wise men of Greece, and were in like manner Gentiles, born of heathens, and brought up among them, and we have no Reason to think that they were themselves less of Heathens than several of the Grecian Philosophers; at least before they were the subjects of that Inspiration that moved them to follow the star that led them to Christ.

Pharaoh and his Chief Butler and Baker were the subjects of a sort of Inspiration in the dreams they had; for it is Evident those dreams were divine Revelations; as were Nebuchadnezzar's dreams. He, though a Heathen, and a very wicked man, and a Great Idolater, yet had a Revelation concerning the Messiah, and his future Kingdom, In his dream of the great Image, and the stone cut out of the mountain without Hands.

If it be objected, that, if we suppose some of the Heathen Philosophers to have Truths suggested to them by the Inspiration of the Spirit of God, we must suppose that God gave those Revelations without giving with Them any certain Evidences by which others, to whom they declared them might determine them to be such, or by which they might be obliged to regard and receive them as such: Allowing this to be the Case, yet a good end might be answered in giving those Revelations nevertheless. Though they could be no Rule to the heathen, among whom they lived, yet they might be of use these three ways.

1. They might dispose the Heathen nations, as they had occasion, to converse with the Jews, and to be informed of the Revelations and Prophecies that they had among them, to attend the more to them, and to enquire into them, and their Evidences.

2. They might prepare the Gentile nations, that had among them the Records of those sayings of their most noted and famous wise men, to receive the Gospel when God's Time came for its promulgation among those nations, by disposing them the more diligently and impartially to attend to it.

3. They may be of Great Benefit to the Christian Church, ages after they were delivered; as they serve as a Confirmation of the great Truths of Christianity.

4. We know not what Evidence God might give to the men themselves that were the Subjects of these Inspirations, that they were divine, and were true; (as we know not what evidence was given to the wise men of the East of the divinity of their Revelations;) and so we know not of how great Benefit the truths suggested might be to their own souls."

APPENDIX I.

B. END OF THE CREATION.

"*g g. Religion.* Tis very certain that God did not create the world for nothing. Tis most certain that if there were not intelligent beings in the world, all the world would be without an end at all; for senseless matter, in whatever excellent order it is placed, would be useless, if there were no intelligent beings at all, neither God nor others; for, what would it be good for? So, certainly, senseless matter would be altogether useless, if there was no intelligent being but God, for God could neither receive good himself, nor communicate good. What would this vast universe of matter placed in such excellent order, and governed by such excellent rule be good for if there was no intelligence that could know anything of it? Wherefore it necessarily follows that intelligent beings are the end of the creation; though their end must be to behold and admire the doings of God, and magnify him for them, and to contemplate his glories in them. Wherefore religion must be the end of the creation, the great end, the very end. If it were not for this all those vast bodies, we see ordered with so excellent skill, so acceptable to the surest rules of proportion, according to such laws of gravity and motion would be all vanity, or good for nothing, and to no purpose at all, for religion is the very business, the noble business of intelligent beings. And for this end God has placed us on this earth. If it were not for men, this world would be altogether in vain, with all the curious workmanship of it, and accoutrements about it. It follows from this that we must be immortal.

The world had as good have been without us, as for us to be a few minutes and then be annihilated. If we are not to own God's works to his glory, and only glorify him a

APPENDIX I.

few minutes and then be annihilated and it shall after that be all one to eternity as if we never had been, and be in vain, after we are dead, that we have been once, and then after the earth shall be destroyed it shall be for the future entirely in vain that either the earth or mankind have ever been. The same agreement seem to be used, Isai. xlv. 17, 18."

"*k k. Religion*. Corollary. Since the world would be altogether good for nothing without intelligent beings, so intelligent beings would be altogether good for nothing except to contemplate the Creator. Hence we learn that devotion and not mutual love, charity, justice, beneficence, etc., are the highest end of man, and devotion is his principal business; for all justice, beneficence, etc., are good for nothing without it, or to no purpose at all, for those duties are only for the advancement of the great business, to assist mutually each other to it."

"*l l. Religion*. It may be said, If religion be really the very business of man, for which God made him, it is a wonder it is no more natural to them; the world in general learnd and unlearnd say little about it, they are very awkward at it; as if it were contrary to their nature. I answer, Tis no wonder, because Sin has brought them down nearer to the beast, a sort of animals uncapable of religion at all."

"87. *Happiness*. 'Tis evident that the end of man's creation must needs be happiness from the motive of God's creating the world, which could be nothing else but his goodness. If it be said that the end of man's creation might be that he might manifest his power, wisdom, holiness, or justice; so I say too; But the question is, Why God would make known his power, wisdom, etc. What could move him to will that there should be some beings that might know his power, and wisdom? It could be nothing else but his goodness. This is the question : What moved God to exercise and make known these attributes. We are not speaking of subordinate ends, but of the ultimate end; of that motive into which all others may be resolved. 'Tis a very proper question to ask, What attribute moved God to exert a power; but 'tis not proper to ask, What moved God to exert his goodness? for this is the notion of goodness, an inclination to shew goodness. Therefore such a question would be no more proper than this, viz., What inclines God to exert his inclination to exert goodness? which is nonsense; for it is an asking and answering a question in the same words. God's power is shown no otherwise than by his powerfully bringing about some end. The very notion of wisdom is wisely contriving for an end; and if there be no end proposed, whatever is done is not wisdom. Wherefore, if God created the world merely from goodness, every whit of this goodness must necessarily, ultimately terminate in the consciousness of the Creation, for the world is no other way capable of receiving goodness in any measure, but intelligent beings are the consciousness of the world. The end therefore of their creation must necessarily be that they may receive the goodness of God, that they may be happy."

"92. *End of Creation.* How then Can it be said that God has made all things for himself, if it is certain that the highest End of the Creation was the communication of happiness? I answer: That which is done for the Gratifying of a natural inclination of God may very properly be said to be done for God. God takes Complacence in Communicating felicity, and he made all things for this Complacence. His Complacence is this, this is making happiness the End of the Creation. Rev. iv. 11."

APPENDIX I.

"104. *End of the Creation*. We have proved that the end of the creation must needs be happiness and the communication of the goodness of God; and that nothing but the Almighty's inclination to communicate of his own happiness could be the motive to him to create the world; and that man or intelligent being is the immediate object of this goodness, and subject of this communicated happiness. And we have shown also that the Father's begetting of the Son is a complete communication of all his happiness, and so an eternal adequate and infinite exercise of perfect goodness that is completely equal to such an inclination in perfection; why then did God incline further to communicate himself, seeing he had done it infinitely and completely? Can there be an inclination to communicate goodness more than adequately to the inclination? To say so, is to say, that to communicate goodness adequate to the inclination, is not yet adequate, inasmuch as he inclines to communicate further, as in the creation of the world. To this I say, That the Son is the adequate communication of the Father's goodness, and is an express and complete image of him. But yet the Son has also an inclination to communicate himself in an image of his person, that may partake of his happiness, and this was the end of the creation even the communication of the happiness of the Son of God, and this was the only motive herein, even the Son's inclination to this. But God the Father is not the object of this, for the Father is not a communication of the Son, and therefore not the object of the Son's goodness; but men, that is those of them that are holy; as the Son says, Psalm xvi. 2, 3. It is Christ here speaks, as is evident by the following passage. And Man, the consciousness or perception of the creation is the immediate subject of this. Therefore the Church is said to be the completeness of

APPENDIX I.

Christ, Eph. i. 23, As if Christ were not complete without the Church, as having a natural inclination thereto. We are incompleat without that which we have a natural inclination to. The man is incompleat without the woman; She is himself, as Christ is not complete without his spouse. The soul is not complete without the body, because human souls have a natural inclination to dwell in a body: So Ephesians i. and ii. last verses. Prov. viii. 30, 31. First we are told where the Father's delight was, and also the mutual delight of the Son, and then where the Son's delight is in the object of his communication of his goodness. "Then I was by him as one brought up with him, etc." The Son is the fulness of God, and the Church is the fulness of the Son of God.

Corol. 1. Then doubtless he is the only proper and fit person to be the Redeemer of men.

Corol. 2. Therefore they are so nearly united to Christ and shall have such intimate communion with him, shall sit down with him in his throne, even as he is set down in his Father's throne and sit with him in the judgment of the world, and their glory and honour and happiness shall be so astonishingly great, as is spoken of in the Scripture.

Corol. 3. Therefore the Son created and doth govern the world; seeing that the world was a communication of him, and seeing the communicating of his happiness is the end of the world.

Corol. 4. We may learn in what sense Christ says, John xv. 9: As the Father loveth the Son as a communication of himself as begotten in pursuance of his eternal inclination to communicate himself, so the Son of God loveth the Church or the Saints, as the effect of his love and goodness, and natural inclination to communicate himself.

APPENDIX I.

Corol. 5. Hence the meaning of Col. i. 16, 17, 18. In this verse there is a trinity, an image of the eternal trinity; wherein Christ is the everlasting Father, and believers are his Seed, and the Holy Spirit, or comforter, is the third person in Christ, being his delight and love flowing out towards the Church. In believers the Spirit and delight of God being communicated unto them flows out towards the Lord Jesus Christ, vid. note on Dan. ix. 25, Mark xiv. 3, and Gen. xxviii. 11, 12.

Corol. 6. Hence we may plainly percieve how these expressions of the Lord Jesus are to be understood, John. xvii. 21, 22, 23, 24, John xiv. 20; These sayings at first seem like nothing but words carelessly cast together, very abstruse and dark, but yet we may here see and know what he meant. Many other of Christ's speeches may receive light from hence; the meaning of the apostle John's gospel and epistles particularly, and many passages through the whole Bible.

Corol. 7. How glorious is the gospel that reveals to us such things.

Corol. 8. Hence we see why it is most suitable and proper that the Son of God should have the immediate management of the affairs of the church, and that it should be this person of the Trinity that has all along manifested himself by the visible tokens of his presence to the antediluvians, the Patriarchs and Israelites."

"197. *Christian Religion.* It seems to me exceeding Congruous and the highest manner Consentaneous that a God, a being of infinite Goodness and love, who, it is evident from mere Reason, Created the world for this very End, to make the Creation happy in his love: I say it seems exceeding Congruous, that he should Give to the Creature the highest sort of Evidence or Expression of love. For why should not that love, which is infinitely

APPENDIX I.

higher than any other and the love of a being infinitely more excellent, of which other love is but the emanation and shadow; why should not that love have the highest and most noble manifestations and the surest Evidences? Now we know that the highest sort of manifestations and evidence of love is expence for the beloved. How much soever the lover Gives, or Communicates to the beloved, yet, if he is at no expence himself, there is not that high and noble expression of love as if otherwise. Now I Can Clearly and distinctly concieve how the Giving of Christ should have all that in it, that Renders it every way an equal, and like, and perfectly equivalent expression of love, as the greatest expence in a lover; as I have shown elsewhere. And this is a way that is exceeding noble and excellent, and agreeable to the Glorious Perfections of God. But no other way can be Concieved of; and they that deny the Christian Religion Can Pretend no other; and if they do 'tis impossible they should think of any in any measure so exalted, noble, and excellent."

"243. *Glory of God.* The first part of the xvii. Chap. of John, and the 18 verse of the xii. Chap., and Isai. xlviii. 11, and Isai. xlii. 8, and many other such passages of Scripture, make me think that God's glory is a good, independent of the happiness of the creature; that it is a good absolutely and in itself and not merely as subordinate to the Creature's real good; nor not merely because it is the Creature's highest good: a good that God seeks, (if I may so speak) not merely as he seeks the Creature's happiness, but for itself; that he seeks absolutely, as an independent, ultimate good. And many passages in the Old Testament that seem to speak as if the end of his doing this or that was his honour's sake, or his name's sake; though it still appears to me exceedingly plain that to Communicate goodness is likewise an absolute good,

APPENDIX I.

and what God seeks for itself, and that the very being of God's goodness necessarily supposes it; for to make happy is not goodness, if it be done purely for another superior end."

"247. *Glory of God*. For God to glorify himself is to discover himself in his works, or to communicate himself in his works, which is all one. For we are to remember that the world exists only mentally; so that the very being of the world implies its being perceived, or discovered. Or otherwise, for God to glorify himself, is, in his acts *ad extra*, to act worthy of himself, or to act excellently. Therefore God does not seek his own glory because it makes him the happier to be honoured and highly thought of, but because he loves to see himself, his own excellencies and glories appearing in his works: He loves to see himself communicated. And it was his inclination to communicate himself, that was a prime motive of his creating the world. His own glory was the ultimate end; himself was his end; that is himself communicated. The very phrase *the glory* seems naturally to signify Glory is a shining forth, an effulgence. So the glory of God is the shining forth, or effulgence of his perfections, or the communication of his perfections; for effulgence is the communication of light. For this reason that brightness, whereby God was wont to manifest himself in the wilderness, and in the tabernacle and temple, was called *God's glory*. So the brightness of the sun, moon, and stars is called their glory; I Cor. xv. 41, John i, 14. We beheld his *glory*, that is his *brightness*, in his transfiguration. II Peter i. 17, Heb. i. 3, Rev. xviii, 1, that is *brightness*. Rev. xxi. 11, verse 23. So that the glory of God is *the shining forth* of his perfections; and the world was created, that they might shine forth; that is that they might be communicated."

APPENDIX I.

"271. *End of the Creation.* It is indeed a condecent thing, that God should be the Ultimate End of the creation, as well as the Cause; that in creating he should make himself his end, that he should in this respect be *omega* as well as *alpha*. and the Scripture saith, "God hath made all things for himself;" and this may be, and yet the reason of his creating the world be his propensity to goodness; and the communication of happiness to creatures be the end. It perhaps was thus: God created the world for his Son, that he might prepare for him a spouse or bride to bestow his love upon, so that the mutual joys between this bride and bridegroom are the end of the creation. God is really happy in loving his creatures; because in so doing he as it were glorifies a natural propensity in the divine nature, viz., goodness. Yea, and he is really delighted in the love of his creatures, and in their glorifying him, because he loves them, not because he needs; for he could not be happy therein, were it not for his love and goodness. Col. i, 16, "All things were made by him, and for him;" that is for the Son."

"332. *End of the Creation.*" The great and universal End of God's creating the world was to communicate Himself. God is a communicative being. His communication is really only to intelligent beings. The communication of Himself to their understandings is His glory and the communication of Himself with respect to their wills, the enjoying *faculty is their happiness.* God created the world for the shining forth of his excellency and for the flowing forth of his happiness. It dont make God the happier to be praised, but it is a becoming and condecent and worthy thing for infinite and supreme excellency so to do."

"445. *End of the Creation.* There is a necessity of

APPENDIX I.

supposing that the exercise of God's goodness, or the Communication of his happiness is not merely a subordinate End, but stands in the Place of an Ultimate End; though there is no necessity of supposing it the only ultimate end. But if God's making his Glory to appear be an ultimate end, this must stand not in subordination to it, but fellow to it, and in the same Rank with it; for to suppose that God's Communication of Goodness is wholly subordinate to some other End, is to suppose that it is not from God's Goodness. That which is Done by any being Entirely in subordination to some other End, or that is not done at all for the sake of itself; that is wholly and only for some other thing, that is more ultimately in view. The attribute or disposition, that excites to that action, is wholly that which seeks that more ultimate end. Thus if God makes the Creature happy, only for a further end, viz., that he may manifest his own perfections by it; then his making the Creature happy is not Indeed from his goodness, or his disposition to communicate good, but wholly from the attribute or disposition of the divine nature, whereby he is disposed to shew forth his own excellency. It is not consistent with the nature of Goodness to be wholly moved and excited by something else that is not Goodness.

If it be said that God Communicates good to the creature only to manifest that Part of his essential Glory, viz., his Goodness, this implies a Great absurdity; for it supposes that God is good only to manifest his own goodness, which goodness is only an Inclination to manifest his glory this way. So that now it Comes to this, that God is Good in order to manifest his Inclination that he has to manifest his Inclination to Communicate good. He Communicates that he may glorify his goodness, which goodness itself is nothing else but an inclination to communicate good for this end, viz., to glorify his inclination to communicate good to this end. And so we may run to Endless nonsense.

If God is Good only to manifest the Glory of his Goodness, then this would be that Glory which was manifested, even his Inclination to manifest his own glory. God has an Inclination to manifest his own Glory, and the Glory which he manifests is this, viz., his disposition to manifest his own Glory; for his Goodness is nothing else, if the sole ultimate end of communicating Good be to Glorify himself or to shew forth the glory of his goodness. Surely God's Glory, that is to be manifested, must be Considered as something Prior to his disposition or design to manifest it. God's Inclining or designing or exerting himself to show his glory, surely, is not that very Glory which he shows: the Glory must be something else besides the manifestation of it.

You will say, Why may not the same be said of God's Justice; why can't the exercise of that be argued to be an ultimate End of the creation? I answer, That when the world is already Created, merely the Glorifying his Justice Cannot be the only motive to his acting Justly; though the Glorifying that attribute might be the motive for his giving himself occasion for the exercise of that attribute by making the Creatures.

Indeed the glory of God cannot be Considered as the Proper end of God's acts of Justice; for if it be tis the glory of his justice is the End, which will Imply those absurdities mentioned concerning God's Goodness being altogether for the glory of his goodness.

A view to the Glorifying of God's Justice is not the sole motive to God's acting Justly when there is occasion; for he acts Justly, because tis agreeable to his nature, and he delights so to do. God's glorifying himself

APPENDIX I.

might be his End in Giving himself occasion for the exercise of his Justice.

So that although God's Glorifying and Communicating himself were the sole Ends for which he created the world; yet they cannot be Properly Considered as the sole ends of All that God does in the world. Thus God when he speaks the truth to his Creatures the sole motive to his speaking the truth, when he does speak, (is not to glorify his truth;) for tis impossible that he should speak anything else: he speaks the truth, because he delights in truth for its own sake.

But the attribute of Justice, or a Just disposition of the Divine nature cannot be directly the motive to God's Creating the world, as his Goodness may. For a Just disposition has for its object only being, existing either in act, or design. It is absurd to suppose that an inclination to do Justice, upon all occasions, should Properly be his motive to Give Creatures being that there may be occasion (to exercise it;) for that is not any part of the notion we have of Justice — a disposition to make occasions for the exercise of Justice. It must be some other disposition that does that; and in God, it is his disposition to cause his attributes to shine forth, or to Glorify himself. But now Goodness, or an Inclination to Communicate Good, has merely possible being as much its proper object, as actual, or designed, being. A disposition to Communicate Good will move a being to make the occasion for the Communication; and Indeed Giving being is one part of the Communication. If God be in himself Disposed to Communicate himself, he is therein disposed to make the Creatures to communicate himself to; because he can't do what he is in himself disposed to do without it. God's Goodness is not an Inclination to Communicate himself, as occasion shall offer, or a

APPENDIX I.

disposition, conditionally, to Communicate himself; but absolutely.

But God's Just and Righteous disposition is only his disposition to act Justly upon every occasion. If God be in himself just that supposes no more than that he will certainly act Justly, whenever there is occasion for his being concerned with the rights or deserts of any. It dont Imply in its nature a disposition to make occasion for it. If God be disposed to make occasions for the exercise of his attributes, that must be only because he is disposed to cause his excellencies to shine forth, or to glorify himself. Vid. 461. Vid. note on the cxxxvi Psalm."

" 448. *End of Creation.* God is glorified within himself these two ways.

1. By appearing, or being manifested to himself in his own perfect Idea; or in his Son, who is the brightness of his glory.

2. By enjoying and delighting in himself, by flowing forth in infinite Love and Delight towards himself; or in his Holy Spirit.

So God glorifies himself towards the creatures also two ways.

1. By appearing to them; being manifested to their understanding.

2. In communicating himself to their hearts, and in their rejoicing and delighting in, and enjoying, the manifestations which he makes of himself.

They both of them may be called his glory in the more extensive sense of the word, viz., his shining forth, or the going forth of his excellency, beauty and essential glory, *ad extra*. By one way it goes forth towards their understandings, by the other it goes forth towards their wills or hearts. God is glorified not only by his glory's being

APPENDIX I.

seen, but by its being rejoiced in. When those that see it delight in it, God is more glorified, than if they only see it. His glory is then received by the whole soul, both by the understanding and by the heart. God made the world that he might communicate, and the creature receive, his glory; and that it might [be] received both by the mind and heart. He that testifies his *views* or *idea* of God's glory, does not glorify God so much, as he that testifies also his *approbation* of it, and his *delight* in it. Both those ways of God's glorifying himself came from the same cause, viz., the overflowing of God's internal glory, or an inclination in God to cause his internal glory to flow out *ad extra*. What God has in view in either of them, either in his manifesting his glory to the understanding or [his] communication of it to the heart, is not that he may receive but that he go forth. The main end of his shining forth is, not that he may have his rays reflected back to himself, but that the rays may go forth. And this [is] very consistent with what we are taught of God's being the Alpha, and Omega, the first and the last. God made all things; and the end for which all things are made, and for which they are disposed, and for which they work continually, is that God's glory may shine forth and be received. From him all creatures come, and in him their well being consists. God is all their beginning, and God, received, is all their end. From him, and to him, are all things; they are all from him, and they are all to be brought to him; but it is not that they may add to him, but that God might be received by them. The damned indeed are not immediately to God, but they are ultimately; they are to the glorified saints and angels, and they to God, that God's glory may be manifested in them unto the vessels of mercy.

It is said that God hath made all things for himself;

APPENDIX I.

and in the Revelation it is said they are created for God's pleasure; that is they are made that God may in them have occasion to fulfil his good pleasure in manifesting and communicating himself. In this God takes delight, and for the sake of this delight God creates the world, but this delight is not properly from the creature's communication to God, but in his to the creature; it is a delight in his own act.

Let us explain the matter how we will, there is no way that the world can be for God save than so for It can't be so for him, as that he can receive anything from the creature.

"553. *End of the Creation.* There are many of the divine attributes, that, if God had not created the world, never would have had any exercise: the power of God, the Wisdom of God, the prudence and contrivance of God, the goodness and mercy, and grace of God, and the justice of God. It is fit that the divine attributes should have exercise. Indeed God knew as perfectly that there were those attributes fundamentally in himself before they were in exercise as since. But as God he delights in his own excellency and glorious perfections, so he delights in the exercise of those perfections. It is true that there was from eternity that act in God, *within himself,* and *towards himself,* that was the exercise of the same perfection of his nature. But it was not the same kind of exercise; it virtually contained it, but there was not explicitly the same exercise of his perfection. God, who delights in the exercise of his own perfection, delights in all the kinds of its exercise. That eternal act or energy, of the divine nature *within him* whereby he infinitely loves and delights in himself, I suppose does imply, fundamentally, goodness and grace towards creatures, if there be that occasion, which infinite wisdom

APPENDIX I.

sees fit. But God, who delights in his own perfection, delights in seeing those exercises of his perfection explicitly in being, that are fundamentally implied."

"662. *End of the Creation. Glory of God.* It may be enquired Why God would have the exercises of his perfections and expressions of His glory known, and published abroad.

Answer, It was meet that His attributes and perfections should be expressed; it was the will of God that they should be expressed and should shine forth; but if the expressions of his attributes are not known they are not expressions; the very being of the expression depends on the perception of created understandings; and so much the more as the expression is known, so much the more it is."

"1082. *End of the Creation.* The glory of the Lord in scripture seems to signify the excellent brightness and fulness of God, and especially as spread abroad, diffused, and as it were enlarged: or, in one word, the excellency of God flowing forth. This was represented in the Shechinah of old. Here, by the excellency of God, I would be understood of everything in God in any respect excellent, all that is great and good in the Deity; including the excellent sweetness, and blessedness that is in God, and the infinite fountain of happiness that the Deity is possessed of, that is called the fountain of life, the water of life, the river of God's pleasures, God's light, etc. The flowing forth of the ineffably bright and sweet effulgence of the Shechinah, represented the flowing out and communicating of this as well as the manifestation of his majesty and beauty; joy and happiness is represented in scripture as often by light, as by water, fountains, streams, etc.—And the communication of God's happiness is represented by the flowing out of

APPENDIX I.

sweet light from the Shechinah, as well as by the flowing forth [of] a stream of delights, and the diffusing of the holy oil, called the fulness of God's house, Ps. xxxvi, 7, 8, 9.

A fountain in diffusing itself abroad in streams, and the holy anointing oil in diffusing itself in a sweet odour, are, in a scripture sense, glorified and magnified, as well as the lamps in the temple by diffusing abroad their light.

Happiness is very often in scripture called by the name of glory, or included in that name, in scripture. God's eternal glory includes his blessedness; and when we read of the glorifying of Christ, and the glory which the Father has given him, it includes his heavenly joy. And so, when we read of the glory promised to or conferred on the saints, and of their being glorified, their unspeakable happiness is a main thing intended. Their joy is full of glory, and they are made happy in partaking of Christ's glory: the fulness of the saints' happiness is the riches of God's glory in the saints. Therefore the diffusing the sweetness and blessedness of the divine nature is God's glorifying himself, in a scripture sense, as well as his manifesting his perfection to their understandings. The beams, that flow forth from the infinite fountain of light and life, don't only carry light, but life, with them; and therefore this light is called the light of life, as the beams of the sun have both light and warmth, and do both enlighten and quicken, and so bless, the face of the earth.

This twofold way of the Deity's flowing forth *ad extra*, answers to the twofold way of the Deity's proceeding *ad intra*, in the proceeding and generation of the Son, and the proceeding and breathing forth of the Holy Spirit; and indeed is only a kind of second proceeding of the same persons: their going forth *ad extra*, as before they proceeded *ad intra*."

APPENDIX I.

"1151. *End of the Creation.* It is no just objection against God's aiming at glorifying himself, as one way of that flowing out, or beaming forth of the infinite good that is to be considered under the notion of a last end of God's works; that this adds nothing to God's happiness; any more than it is a just objection against his Communicating his happiness to his creatures being aimed at by him as his last end; for the creature's happiness does not properly add anything to God's happiness, any more than God's being glorified in the view of the creature, and by the creature, adds something to God's happiness. It is true, God delights in communicating his happiness to the creature, as therein he exercises a perfection of his nature, and does that which is condecent, amiable, and beautiful, and so enjoys himself and his own perfection in it, as his perfection is exercised in it. So, in like manner, he delights in glorifying himself, as it is in itself condecent and beautiful that infinite brightness and glory should shine forth, and it is a part of the perfection of God to seek it.

These two ways of the divine good beaming forth, are agreeable to the two ways of the divine essense flowing out, or proceeding from eternity within the godhead, in the person of the Son and Holy Spirit: the one, in an expression of his glory, in the idea or knowledge of it; the other, the flowing out of the essence in love and joy. It is condecent that, correspondent to these proceedings of the divinity *ad intra*, God should also flow forth *ad extra*.

The one last end of all things may be expressed, thus: It is, that the infinite good might be communicated; that it might be communicated to, or rather in, the understanding of the creature, which communication is God's declarative glory; and that it might be communicated to the other faculty (usually, though not very express-

APPENDIX I.

ively, called the Will) which communication is the making the creature happy in God, as a partaker of God's happiness."

"1218. *End of the Creation, Glory of God*, etc. It can't be properly said that the end of God's creating of the world is twofold; or that there are two parallel co-ordinate ends of God's creating the world : one, to exercise his perfections ad extra; another, to make his creatures happy. But all is included in one, viz., God's exhibiting his perfections, or causing his essential glory to be exercised, expressed and communicated ad extra. Tis true that we must suppose that, prior to the creature's existence, God seeks occasion to exercise his goodness, and opportunity to communicate happiness, and that this is one end whereby he gives being to creatures ; and so we must conceive this prior to the creature's existence. He seeks occasion to exercise other attributes of his nature, that can have none but creatures for their objects ; as his justice, his faithfulness, his wisdom, etc. But a disposition to seek opportunity and occasion for the exercise of goodness towards those that now have no being, and so a being disposed to give being to creatures, that there may be such an opportunity, is not the same attribute that we commonly call Goodness ; any more than a disposition to seek opportunity or occasion to exercise justice, and so to give being to creatures that there may be such occasion, is not the same attribute that we call Justice. God seeks occasion for the exercise of one and the other of those attributes, by giving existence to beings that may be capable objects of their exercise, in the same manner, and for one common reason, viz., because it is in itself fit and suitable that these attributes of God should be exerted, and should not be eternally dormant. Tis true tis from an excellent disposition of the heart of

APPENDIX I.

God, that God seeks occasion to exercise his goodness and bounty, and also his Wisdom, Justice, Truth; and this in one word is a disposition to glorify himself, according to the Scripture sense of such an expression, or a disposition to express and communicate himself ad extra.

I know there is an inconsistency in supposing that God inclines to exercise goodness, and do Good to others, meerly for the sake of the Honour of his Goodness; for the very notion of Goodness is an Inclination of Heart to do good to others. And therefore, the Existence of such an Inclination must be conceived of as prior to an Inclination to Honour it. There must first be an Inclination of Heart to do good, before God desires to honour that Inclination. So in like manner it is an inconsistence to suppose that God is inclined to Exercise Justice, and do justly, only for the sake of the Honour of his Justice; for Justice itself is an Inclination to do justly, which must exist before God is inclined to honour it. Therefore God's glorifying Himself — that glorifying Himself, which is the End of the creation — is a different thing from properly seeking his Honour.

They, that suppose God's inclination to make occasions for the doing Good, or communicating Happiness, by giving being to capable subjects of it, to be what is properly called God's Goodness, seem to have a Notion of a bountiful disposition in the Heart of God, disposed to increase the sum of Happiness, which is to be found in the universality of Existence. But there is no such Thing. Man's Benevolence and Bounty, taking his own Good, and the Good of the Person benefitted by Him together, increases the sum of Good; and therefore tis more easy to conceive of a benevolent Disposition in a Creature wishing for the being of new subjects of Kindness, because the Goodness of his Nature causes Him to love to see a great deal of Happiness.

APPENDIX I.

But God sees no more by making creatures that they may be happy.

He hath in his Son an adequate object for all the desires of this kind that are in his Heart, and in his Infinite Happiness, he sees as much Happiness as can be when new beings are made that are infinitely less, and there is opportunity to do them good, God sees not the sum of happiness increased.

The more proper Notion signified by all such words as Goodness, Kindness, Bounty, Favour, Grace, etc., includes Love, Benevolence or Good will, but this is not properly Love or Good will that has the Existence of the object loved first supposed. A disposition to make an object that it may be loved, and that we may have good will towards must be prior to another, and properly distinct from Love and Goodwill itself. It may be an excellent Quality, but it must be Quality of some other denomination: if it be called Goodness and Grace it must be in a less proper sense. To desire new beings to communicate happiness to 'em, especially without increasing the sum of Happiness, dont agree with the notion mankind have of Goodness, Benevolence, Grace, etc. Men may call this disposition in the Heart of God by the name of Goodness, if they please; but tis properly referred to another Perfection of which it is one sort of exercise; viz., the disposition that is in the Infinite Fountain of Good and of Glory, and Excellency, to shine forth, or flow out; which shining forth or flowing out of God's infinite fulness, is called God's Glory in Scripture.

Indeed God, in making the creature happy, seems as it were to express, or exhibit himself *ad extra*, two ways. Not only does one of his perfections exercise itself in it, viz., his Goodness; but there is something of God actually communicated, some of that Good that is in God,

APPENDIX I.

that the creature hereby has communion in, viz., God's Happiness: the creature partakes of the happinesss of God, at least an image of it. And we must therefore conceive that there is a disposition in God not only to exercise his attributes and perfections in this, but also to communicate of his divine good. But then it is to be considered that God does not only communicate of happiness, but also his holiness, and his understanding, and power, or an image of these; and we must conceive that there is truly a disposition in God to communicate of these, as well as his happiness; which general disposition, though in itself excellent, seems to be a disposition besides the goodness of God, or at least is called so in a less proper sense, and in a more extensive sense than that which is more frequently called God's goodness. But although there are several kinds of good in God, that are communicated, and though according to our manner of conceiving things there are two ways of God's exhibiting himself *ad extra:* 1. His perfections that we conceive to be an active nature are exercised *ad extra;* as his power, wisdom, justice, goodness, holiness; 2. The Good that is in him is communicated ad extra; and, though this good be of various kinds according to our manner of conceiving, yet as all this good that is in God, of whatever kind, belongs to his essential glory and brightness, and there is the same fitness that each part of this brightness or glory should shine forth in every possible way, and be both exercised and communicated, and that all this good should flow out, and that God is disposed that each part should do so, may well be referred to one general disposition, and the effect may well be called by one name, viz., God's Glory: $\Delta o\xi a$. כבוד.

Both these dispositions of exerting himself and communicating himself, may be reduced to one, viz., a dis-

APPENDIX I.

position effectually to exert himself, or to exert himself in order to an effect. That effect is the communication of himself, or himself ad extra, which is what is called his glory. This communication is of two sorts: the communication that consists in understanding or idea, which is summed up in the knowledge of God; and the other is in the will consisting in love and joy, which may be summed up in the love and enjoyment of God. Thus that which proceeds from God ad extra is agreeable to the twofold subsistences which proceed from him ad intra which is the Son, and the Holy Spirit: the Son being the idea of God, or the knowledge of God; and the Holy Ghost, which is the love of God and joy in God.

Although the things which God inclines to and aims at, are in some respects two, viz., exercising or exerting the perfections of his nature, and the effect of that, viz., communicating himself; yet these may be reduced to one, viz., God's exerting himself in order to the effect. The exertion and the effect ought not to be separated, as though they were two ends; one is so related to the other, and they are so united that they are most properly taken together as one end, and the object of one inclination in God; for tis not an ineffectual exertion that God aims at, or inclines to, and God in aiming at these makes himself his end. Tis Himself exerted, and Himself communicated; and both together are what is called God's *Glory*. The end, or the thing which God attains, is Himself, in two respects. He himself flows forth; and He Him[self] is pleased and gratified: for God's pleasure all things are, and were created.

God has made intelligent creatures capable of being concerned in these effects, as being the willing active subjects, or means; and so they are capable of actively promoting God's glory. And this is what they ought to make their ultimate end in all things."

APPENDIX I.

"1266. Glory of God, the End Of the Creation. God's Glory, as it is spoken of in scripture, as the End of all God's works, is, in one word, The Emanation of that Fulness of God, that is from Eternity in God, *ad extra*, and towards those Creatures that are capable of being sensible and active objects of such an Emanation. It consists in communicating Himself to those two Faculties of the Understanding and will ; by which Faculties it is, that Creatures are sensible and active objects, or subjects, of divine Emanations, and communications.

God communicates himself to the understanding in the manifestation that is made of the divine Excellency ; and the understanding, Idea, or view, which Intelligent creatures have of it. He communicates his Glory and Fulness to the wills of sensible, willing, active beings in their rejoicing in the manifested Glory of God; in their admiring it ; in their loving God for it, and being in all respects affected and disposed suitably to such Glory, and their exercising and expressing those affections and dispositions wherein consists their Praising and Glorifying God ; and in their being themselves holy, and having the Image of this Glory in their Hearts, and as it were reflecting it as a Jewel does the Light of the Sun, and as it were partaking of God's Brightness ; and in their being Happy in God, whereby they partake of God's Fulness of Happiness.

This twofold Emanation or communication of the divine Fulness *ad extra* is answerable to the twofold Emanation or going forth of the Godhead *ad intra ;* wherein the internal and Essential Glory and Fulness of the Godhead consists : viz., the Proceeding of the Eternal Son of God, God's Eternal Idea and infinite understanding and wisdom, and the Brightness of his Glory, whereby his Beauty and Excellency appears to Him ; and

APPENDIX I.

the Proceeding of the Holy Spirit, or the Eternal will, Temper, disposition of the Deity, the infinite Fulness of God's Holiness, Joy, and Delight."

"1275. *That Glory of God*, that is the *End of God's Works*, is not only a manifestation of his Excellency, but a communication of his happiness. Goodwin's Works, Vol. 1, Part 2, p. 246, on Happiness. Words, Eph. ii, 7, "It implies that God will rejoice over you in glorifying of you. It imports that he will not do it merely to show his riches, as Ahasuerus made a feast and invited all his nobles, to show the riches of his glorious kingdom. God indeed will bring us to heaven, and show the exceeding riches of his grace; and that is the chiefest end he aims at. But now Ahasuerus did not do this in kindness. But God, as he will there show forth the exceeding riches of his grace, *for the glorifying of it*, so he will do it in all the sweetness and kindness that your souls can desire or expect."

Ibid. p. 250. "It hath been questioned by some, Whether the first moving cause to move God to go forth to save men was the manifesting his own glory, or his kindness and love to men, which he was pleased to take up towards them. I have heard it argued with much appearance of strength, That, however God indeed in the way of saving men carries it as becomes a God, so as his own glory and grace shall have the pre-eminence, yet that which first moved him, that which did give the occasion to him to go forth in the manifestation of himself which else he needed not, was rather kindness to us than his own glory; yet so as if he resolved out of kindness and love to us to manifest himself at all he would do it like a God, and he would show forth the exceeding riches of his grace, as that that alone should be magnified. Now the truth is the text (Eph. ii. 7) compounds the business,

APPENDIX I.

and doth tell us plainly and truly, that the chief end is that God should glorify his own grace. It puts the chief and original end upon the showing forth the exceeding riches of his grace; Yet so as that he hath attempered and conjoined therewith the greatest kindness, the greatest loving affection in the way of manifesting of it, so as in the way of carrying it. It shall appear it is not simply to glorify himself, but out of kindness towards us, he puts that in as that which shall run along with all the manifestation of his own glory. And therefore now he makes in the 4th verse mercy and great love to us, to be as well the fountain and foundation of our salvation as the manifestation of the riches of his grace here."

Ibid. p. 253. "Because the chief and utmost thing that God desireth is the manifestation of the riches of his grace, it argues, that his end of manifesting himself was not wholly for himself, but to communicate unto others why? because grace is wholly communicative. There can be no other interpretation of showing the riches of his grace but to do good unto others. If he had said that the supreme end had been the manifestation of his power and wisdom, it might have imported something he would have gotten from the creature; not by communicating anything unto them, but by manifesting these upon them. He could have showed his power and wisdom upon them, as he hath done upon the men he hath cast into hell and yet have communicated no blessedness to them. No, saith God, My highest and chief end is not so much to get anything from you, but to show forth the riches of my grace towards you. Thus, look at faith which is the highest grace in us; it is merely a receiving grace from God. So take grace, which is the chief thing God would exalt; what is it from God, a mere bestowing, communicating property and attribute. It imports noth-

APPENDIX I.

ing else but a communication unto us. It is well therefore for us, that God hath made the highest end of our salvation in himself (when he will aim at himself too) to be that which shall communicate all to us. It is, saith the text, to show forth the riches of his grace."

Ibid: Part 3, p. 63. " Our allwise and infinitely blessed Lord who had, from everlasting, riches of glorious perfections, which, though he himself knew, and was infinitely blessed in the knowledge of them, though no saint or angel had ever been or ever knew them; yet all these his glorious perfections being crowned with goodness, have made him willing to make known what riches of glory were in him unto some creatures which yet were in Christ. His goodness moved him to it. For Bonum est sui communicatio,—and it is the nature of perfection also to be manifestatio sui. And that not because any perfection is added to it when made known, but that they might perfect others. This set Him upon some ways to make known his riches and his glory to some that should be made happy by it; and to that end he would have saints, (his saints as being beloved of him) unto whom he might as it were unbosom himself, and display all the riches of glory that are in him; into whose laps he might withal pour out all his riches, that they might see his glory, and be glorified in seeing of it. John xvii, 3, 24."

APPENDIX II.

LOAN EXHIBITION

Not the least interesting part of the Bicentenary was the exhibition, in Bartlet Chapel, of many autograph and published writings of Edwards and other objects of historical interest, partly in the possession of the Seminary, and partly loaned by friends for this special occasion. The books were in large part from the Seminary Library, but several of the most interesting came from the Congregational Library of Boston, the Boston Public Library, and the Library of Harvard University. The manuscripts were mainly from the collection of Professor E. C. Smyth. Other objects were loaned by Professor Smyth and Miss Park, of Andover, Dr. H. C. Hovey, of Newburyport, Mrs. A. C. Stone, of Lawrence, and the Rev. Calvin M. Clark, of Haverhill. To all these friends the thanks of the Seminary are hereby extended for their kind co-operation in making the exhibition a success.

The following list includes the most interesting of the objects exhibited, leaving out the books : —

A sketch of the life of Richard Edwards, of Hartford, by his son, the Rev. Timothy Edwards.

Letter from Mrs. Solomon Stoddard to her daughter, Mrs. Timothy Edwards, after the birth of her son, Jonathan.

Letter from the Rev. Timothy Edwards to his son, Jonathan, dated Feb. 13, 1716.

Letter from Rector Cutler, of Yale, to Timothy Edwards, congratulating him on the good qualities of his son, dated June 30, 1719.

APPENDIX II.

Unpublished letter of Edwards to his father, dated at Yale College, March 1, 1721.

Various treatises in manuscript, including, Of the Rainbow; Of Insects, being the first draft of Edwards's account of The Flying Spider; The Flying Spider, and draft of a letter to a gentleman in England accompanying the same; Notes on Science, with specimens of shorthand writing and of illustrative figures; On the Soul; Of Being, written while a college student; Manuscripts relating to Qualifications for Communion, and Prophecies of the Messiah.

Leaves from Edwards's Hebrew Bible, containing his family record.

Notes of sermons preached to the Mohawk Indians in Stockbridge, in January and February, 1751.

Letter to the Rev. Joseph Bellamy, dated Canaan, Nov. 5, 1750, concerning a proposed sale of sheep, occasioned by Edwards's enforced resignation of his Northampton parish.

Numerous letters from the later years of his life.

Notes from which Edwards preached his farewell sermon to the Stockbridge Indians, Jan. 8, 1758, just before his removal to Princeton.

Letter of Dr. Shippen, the attending physician, announcing the death of Edwards to his wife. Written from Princeton, March 22, 1758.

Letter from Mrs. Edwards to her daughter, Susanna, after the death of Edwards. Written April 3, 1758.

A Latin Dictionary belonging to Sarah Pierpont, who became Mrs. Edwards; a piece of her wedding dress; a wrought iron tray, supposed to be one of her wedding presents; the manuscript containing an account of Mrs. Edwards's religious experiences of Jan. 19, 1742, narrated by her to her husband, and recorded by him.

APPENDIX II.

Copy of a Covenant entered into by the people of God at Northampton, March 16, 1741-2; a fragment of the cloth used with the communion service at Northampton during Edwards's pastorate.

Numerous sermons, notes and plans for sermons, showing his shorthand writing, and his economy in making use of newspaper margins, fragments of letters, pulpit notices, proclamations, and especially scraps of paper left by his daughters from their manufacture of fans.

A Note Book of "Things to be particularly enquired into and written upon".

A letter to the Rev. John Erskine of Kirkintilloch, Scotland, in which Edwards speaks of his thoughts of writing on the Freedom of the Will and Moral Agency. It is dated Northampton, Jan. 22, 1746-7.

A silver bowl or porringer, inscribed with the names of its various owners, viz. Pres't Jonathan Edwards, Hon. Timothy Edwards, Phoebe (Edwards) Hooker, Edward W. Hooker, Edward T. Hooker. By will of Edward W. Hooker the porringer must thereafter go to an orthodox Congregational clergyman in direct descent. Loaned by the present owner, the Rev. Calvin M. Clark, of Haverhill.

APPENDIX II.

CONGRATULATORY MESSAGE

To the Committee of Arrangements for celebrating the Bicentenary of the Reverend Jonathan Edwards, M.A.

The Senatus of the Glasgow College of the United Free Church of Scotland have deputed their colleague, the Reverend James Orr, D.D., to represent them at the celebration of the Bicentenary of the celebrated Jonathan Edwards within your theological Seminary. Our Senatus gladly unites with you in doing honour to one of the earliest of renowned American Theologians, whose pre-eminent abilities were recognized in his life-time not only in the land of his birth but throughout Great Britain and Germany, and whose writings, more especially his Treatise on the Freedom of the Will, his work on the Doctrine of Original Sin, and above all his Treatise on the Religious Affections, have taken and must always retain a place among the theological master-pieces of earlier generations.

The Senatus congratulate the Andover Theological Seminary, so justly celebrated among American Schools of Divinity, on this celebration, and they see a peculiar fitness in a Seminary, so well known for its theological activity in the present, summoning around it theologians from all lands to do honour to one of the greatest theologians of the past.

The Senatus send cordial fraternal greetings and desire to express every wish for the success of the Meetings to be held on the fifth of October.

In the Name and by the Authority of the Senatus

(signed) THOMAS M. LINDSAY,
Principal.

College of the United Free Church of Scotland,
Glasgow, June 9, 1903.

APPENDIX II.

REPLY TO THE CONGRATULATORY MESSAGE

To the Reverend Thomas M. Lindsay, D.D., Principal of the Glasgow College of the United Free Church of Scotland, Greeting:

The Faculty of Andover Theological Seminary take pleasure in acknowledging the congratulatory message of the Senatus of Glasgow College, received on the occasion of the two-hundredth anniversary of the birth of Jonathan Edwards, to be observed on October fifth. They highly value and cordially reciprocate the fraternal good wishes therein expressed. They also gratefully acknowledge their indebtedness to Glasgow College and the United Free Church of Scotland for the favoring presence in Andover, at the approaching Bicentenary, of an honored representative of modern Scotch Theology, the Reverend Professor James Orr, D.D., whose name lends distinction to the order of proceedings, and whose address is certain largely to enhance their historical value.

Adopted at a meeting of the Faculty, held in Andover, on the sixteenth day of September, Nineteen Hundred and Three.

(signed) CHARLES ORRIN DAY,
President.

www.ingramcontent.com/pod-product-compliance
Lightning Source LLC
Chambersburg PA
CBHW071423160426
43195CB00013B/1781